GALLOP

ALISON BRACKENBURY was born in Lincolnshire in 1953 and studied at Oxford. She now lives in Gloucestershire where she works, as a director and manual worker, in the family metal-finishing business. Her Carcanet collections include *Dreams of Power* (1981), *Breaking Ground* (1984), *Christmas Roses* (1988), *Selected Poems* (1991), *1829* (1995), *After Beethoven* (2000), *Bricks and Ballads* (2004) and *Skies* (2016). Her poems have been included on BBC Radio 3 and 4, and *1829* was produced by Julian May for Radio 3. Her work recently won a Cholmondeley Award.

GALLOP

SELECTED POEMS

Alison Brackenbury

CARCANET

First published in Great Britain in 2019 by
Carcanet
Alliance House, 30 Cross Street
Manchester M2 7AQ
www.carcanet.co.uk

A CIP catalogue record for this book is
available from the British Library.
ISBN 978 1 784106 95 9

Book design by Andrew Latimer
Printed in Great Britain by SRP Ltd, Exeter, Devon

The publisher acknowledges financial
assistance from Arts Council England.

Supported using public funding by
ARTS COUNCIL
ENGLAND

MIX
Paper from
responsible sources
FSC® C014540

Contents

from CHRISTMAS ROSES

from 1829

from AFTER BEETHOVEN

from BRICKS AND BALLADS

from SINGING IN THE DARK

from THEN

from SKIES

GALLOP

My Old

My old are gone; or quietly remain
Thinking me a cousin from West Ham,
Or kiss me, shyly, in my mother's name.
(My parents seem to dwindle too; forget
Neat ending to a sentence they began,
Beginning of a journey; if not yet.)

Cards from village shops were sent to me
With postal orders they could not afford.
They pushed in roots of flowers, carelessly,
And yet they grew; they said a message came
To say the Queen was dead, that bells were heard.
My old are gone into the wastes of dream.

The snow froze hard, tramped down. Old footprints pit
Its smoothness, blackened footprints that I tread
That save me falling, though they do not fit
Exactly, stretching out beyond my sight.
My old are gone from name. They flare instead
Candles: that I do not have to light.

Gallop

An unholy conspiracy
of girls and horses, I admit,
as never being part of it
but riding late and anxiously.
On Sunday when the horses climb the hill
scrambling the dried watercourse to reach
the open field to gallop: all my breath
swells hot inside me as the horses bunch
and pull for mad speed, even my old horse –

'gently!' the leader calls – but they are gone,
hunters, young horses, surging hard ahead,
I rock across the saddle, the wet soil
flung shining past me, and the raking feet
shaking me from saddle as I speak
breathless, kind names to the tossing neck
haul back the reins, watching the widening gap
between my foundered horse and the fast pack,

wondering if I can keep on, why I do this;
and as he falters, my legs tired as his,
I faintly understand this rage for speed:
careless and hard, what do they see ahead,
galloping down spring's white light, but a gate
a neat house, a small lawn, a cage of sunlight?

And pounding slow behind, I wish that I
rode surely as they do but wish I could
tell them what I see in sudden space –
Two flashing magpies rising from the trees,
two birds: good omen; how the massive cloud
gleams and shadows over as they wait,
the horses blown and steaming at shut gates:
disclosing, past their bright heads, my dark wood.

The House

It was the house of childhood, the house of the dark wood,
four-square and safe. It was the second house
at least, to bear its name. The first was burnt: was charred
foundations, hidden by a timber yard.

I knew this in my dream: the house was same
and solid. All its yews, church trees, were strong
red wood of generations. As we came
out in the dusk sight heaved, house, orchard, gone.
Cold in the trembling grass we shivered there.
On open hillside, to the first stars' stare

I watched dark, unsurprised. I could remember
the bombers roaring low above the trees
to reach their high drome, though the war was done.
The house had strained and crumbled.
                                        There is only
                    the old magic, forced out in new ways.
Hard through the dream's cold spring I raised
My house again. My bones and my heart ache
In every joist. The altered rooms are filled
With lovely light: the only house
Which kills in falling, which you must rebuild –

            In new wood boxes, apples there
All winter breathe out sweetness, in cold air.

The Divers' Death

The two dead divers hauled up in their bell
died not from lack of air but the great cold.
The linking cable severed and they fell
fathoms of dark, away from tides that rolled,
from gulls that rode the storm, from sun that warmed
down where the wind dropped; and the hands that cried,
used to much, not this. No breath
deserved the line to break, the spasm, black to death.

And so the dead child, taken quickly out
from white walls, the emptied woman. Or
brain-damaged babies, who can roll about
like small sea-creatures on the padded floor.
Someone washes them and listens for
their cries; they turned their heads when we went near.
But someone might have wished for them a knife
to exorcise the darkness of that life.

Deeper than the bright, fast fishes go
are the great depths that divers cannot kill –
what knife could cut so bitterly? And so
we are love's strange seabirds. We dive there, still.

Because

you dazzled me with cleverness,
mocked the magician, 'Stripped of cheats he can
do no more than you, or anyone.
The doves are tame. He is a shrunken man.
Sleeves of silk handkerchiefs, like crumpled wings
a shiny card hid in his sweating palm,
bright saws which do not cut are all his art.
It is your dull belief which does you harm.'

Your eyes fixed on me. But I climbed the stage
to help his act. Was it the final trick,
because I was so frightened of your rage?
Because I disobeyed you or because
all my art was gone in loving you
icy and true silver ran my tears,
dazzled, by the light we vanished through.

Derby Day: An Exhibition

The great Stubbs' picture of the great Eclipse
Hangs in the corner it defies,
Effortless. The great are luminous.
Orbed flanks shine solid, amber, having won.
A gold-red horse called Hermit won, and broke
The wild Earl of Hastings, who had flung
Woods and fields against. How can Eclipse
Comfort those eclipsed, who never won?

The young Fred Archer, with a boy's sad face,
Shot himself, sick dizzy on the edge.
He won six flaring Derbys. Not that one
In which a woman sprang beneath the rail.
In thudding dark, pain tore all colours; died.

And yet a brilliant day. Do not mistake:
That which we do best kills us. Horse and man
Amber in the mist of downs, sea-shore,
The spring of wave, glow greatly. They survive.

These Are the Colours

These are the colours. New, cold blue
which glints between the drifting packs,
the wasted dark of the long day,

pure snow, which fills and freezes in our tracks.

This is the region where the ships are caught
where gold-billed swans die heaving in the ice
to which the lode-stone sings with human voice

this song I sail into your northern eyes.

Kingdoms

Gold, edged with green, the peacock's eyes
ducked and shimmered past my head
to see the young Athenians
who could not leap the bull, lie dead.
Their ended screams still twist my sleep
become the staircase where I run,
of alabaster pale as milk
in courtyards where the black bull shone
his high horns lashed with reddening silk.

Black, pierced with grey, pricks morning's leaves,
where all the headdresses lie dark
crushed now in rough volcano ash;
where now we sleep in shelters, cracks
in painted stones: in fear I brush
for morning's sticks through the deep wood.

A young black bull they would have found
with net, gold rope for sacrifice
stirs through the thicket: I am caught
only in his drowsing eyes:
a smudge of mist. He rubs the grey
smooth trunk; blinks sleep, walks slow away.

For pomp and cold, twigs crackle: fade.
In a still space I am drawn.
Fire, be moth-wing, grey and gold,
bull and dancer: ash and dawn.

'Yesterday Vivaldi visited me, and sold me some very expensive concertos.'

He had only one tune.
And that
a thin finger on pulses:
of spring and the frost,
                    the quick turn of girls' eyes
a tune

to hold against darkness,
to fret
for trumpet, for lute
for flutes; violins
to silver the shabbiness
of many towns
the fool's bowl, the court coat,
a tune he would give
without sorrow or freedom
again, again

            there is only one tune.

Sell it dearly to live.

The Wood at Semmering

This is a dismal wood. We missed our train.
Leaning on a bench, and happy while
The express, green, like a Personenzug
Slid past us as we sat there with a smile.
Tree draughts blow smells of earth to us and tug
A memory: a sadness, found again.

For in this place the nervous women meet
Summer, summer; watch their fingers shake
To splash a tonic water round the glass.
Where the widow, thin, brown-haired, will take
Her daily walk between the pines; will pass
Small cones and drifting flowers, with numb feet.

Past pale yellow foxgloves, small to ours,
Where harebells darken purple, she steps slow.
The toad-flax opens deeper mouths of gold,
The tiny eye-bright, high white daisies blow.
Rose of chill lips, small cyclamen unfold,
And touch her feet.

              For earth has many flowers.

The Two

do not fear
the golden wings

sun lit their tips
before they fell

all lips meet the shadowed sea
love pity no such ends

your pity fits the careful man
who joined soft wax with feathers well

who fell alone: on a grey shore:
        on whom all love depends.

Intimates

You lived too near the ghosts. For they were kind
dry, warm as snakes you never feared.
Speak now of love to men whose eyes
are moist and cold,
unkind as the true world.

For you are woken now by evening's rain
(a snake would shiver, slip into the dark)
are startled as it smashes on hot land.
The sky-light leaks. Rain pricks against your wrist –
Strange fingers slip the gold ring from your hand.

Two Gardeners

Too far: I cannot reach them: only gardens.
And stories of the roughness of their lives.
The first, an archaeologist, had lost
Her husband to the Great War; never married
Again, but shared her fierce father's house;
Lit oil lamps and humped bright jugs of water
Until he died. We went there selling flags
Stopped at the drive's turn: silenced by her garden.

White water-lilies smoked across her pools.
The trees were hung with musk-roses
Pale as Himalayas; in darker space
Gleamed plants as tall as children, crowned with yellow,
Their name I never learnt. Her friends had found
Smuggled her seeds and lush stalks, from abroad;
While she walked with her father's snapping dog
Or drew the Saxon fields of Lincolnshire.

The other lived in the cold Northern side
Of a farmhouse, split for the farm's workers,
(Where we lived then). Once she had been a maid,
Had two children for love before she married
A quiet man. Away from her dark kitchen
She built a bank, her husband carried soil.
There she grew monkey flowers, red and yellow,
Brilliant as parrots, but more richly soft.
She said I could help plant them, but I dare
Not touch the trembling petals – would not now.
I have sown some. I do not look to see
Such generous gold and scarlet, on dark air.

Both live; I call them gardeners. And I grow
Angry for them, that they might be called
Typically English. They were no more that
Than sun or wind, were wild and of no place.
The roots of light plants touched them for a while
But could not hold them: when they moved
They left all plants to strangers

                              in whose dust
The suburbs' wind sucks up white petals round me
To look and see them in their earth-dark shoes
Skirts stained by water, longer yet than ours.

Dazzled by dry streets I touch their hands,
Parted by the sunlight, no man's flowers.

Summer in the Country

'Strawberries', 'raspberries', whisper the letters
Until July is a taste, to hide
In reddened mouths, in fields which feet
Can't flatten, tall, soft throbbed with heat.
Where horses shaking gnats aside
Come slow to hand through the darkening grass

Where seeds fall too, from willow trees
(Rooted in damp, an ancient drain)
White silk clings to my back. I see
Small clouds pass slowly overhead.
Ask me nothing. In harvest fields
Drivers wear masks – cough dust; hear grain
Hiss profit; loss. But in the shade
Pale seed drops lightly over me.

The harvest ends. White webs of cold
Are strung across the sun;
The wind blows now no hint of fruit
but draught, unease, what's done; undone.

Robert Brackenbury

Ancestors are not in our blood, but our heads:
we make history.
Therefore I claim
you, from dark folds of Lincolnshire
who share my name
and died two hundred years ago
you, man, remembered there
for doing good: lost, strange and sharp you rise
like smoke: because it was your will
all letters, papers, perish when you died.

Who burnt them? Wife or daughter, yawning maid
poked down the struggling blackness in the grate
or walked slow, to the place where leaves were burnt,
the white air, winter's. Slips of ash
trembled on the great blue cabbage leaves:
O frozen sea.

Why Robert, did
you hate the cant of epitaph so much?
leave action to be nothing but itself:
the child who walked straight-legged, the man
whose house no longer smoked with rain, and yet
(soft scent of grass in other men's archives)
your name, to linger; did you trust
that when all shelves, all studies fell to ash
your kindness still might haunt our wilderness
a hand that plucks at us, a stubborn leaf
twitching before rain
                              or did despair
turn: whisper there how you were young

to burn and change your world: not enough done,
from that you turned
to silence and a shadowed wall; unkind
to family, to wife and to that maid:
who buried you, for love, in Christian ground.

I think that you had ceased to trust in knowledge.
You did not want the detail of your life
wrapped round us like a swaddling cloth; passed, known,
to shadow over us like a great tree.
The crumbling, merging soil, the high rooks
cawing out the black spring are for you;
now we must speak and act: make day alone.

In one thing I'll be resolute as you.
In white day in the thawing grass I'll burn
one letter, then the bundles; stare
at the cracked silvering of walnut bark:
and see what, in that grace? Not you,
your eyes of frozen dark.

Snatch back the half-charred letter! In the icy
blue, wasted leaves watch silent the unmaking
flames crumble white

too like a God forsaking
the heart to ash.

And though I made you, though
I should ask nothing of you
I will turn against you, bitter
as the girl's mouth in the garden
tasting winter, ashes: glow
of fire that cannot warm us
or ever quite betray
smoke that twists the cold hand
       in shapes I do not know.

An Orange of Cloves

Clove-scent: the dark room where the lovers lie
A closet smelling both of must and musk,
Which makes the head faint: rawer and more old
Than pale-flowered stocks which scent the dusk.

Caverns of dark I entered first: I thought
I have danced here, and to a golden lute.
Branched velvet, rushes, gallows in the sunlight –

sense shudders till it glimpses in a space
The great sharp-scented tree, its flowers, its fruit
All of a season, beating in the rain;
The orange, cloves cross-cleft; and past the pain,
a dark tree fading, seeding in each face.

Dreams of Power

NOTE

Arbella Stuart (1575–1615) was the orphaned granddaughter of Elizabeth of Hardwick, keeper of Arbella's aunt, the dethroned Mary Stuart. She was briefly married to William Seymour, great-nephew of Lady Jane Grey, and died in the Tower of London.

I. Legends

Five winter days were lit by the slow thaw:
a light space in the window's frost shows us
my grandmothers: King Henry's threadbare niece;
Elizabeth in richest black, who crossed
from merchant's bed to Earl's; unloving looks
must have snicked between them, as they walked
the gold-edged carpets in the smoking light.
Margaret's son lay coughing in his bed
with the shy girl, my mother, sent 'to nurse'
thrust in the scented room and the doors closed.

The cold of those five days is in my heart:
old eyes appraising and the whispering.
My bed's long curtains with their yellow flowers
hiss serpent's breath, soft perfuming
which they laid round the young Elizabeth
to sweeten her pale boy. He married her;
dolls have no power
                                    although a dark eye saw,
crumpled him in a strong room in the Tower.
Some jewel or promise, in my mother's dress,

undermined his warder for an hour.
And so my life burst in: between damp walls
with awkward coupling on a narrow bed.
I leave with her; duck, from the guard's eyes
down rocking stairs, go down the roofless yard
in a dark softness which the late rain frees
which I know, and the shuddered open body
(down which, the thick cloak pulls)
rises to moon's glitter, floating high.
Above the battlements the young moon swells,
she heaps great tides and yet would not destroy,
shut out day from this high glass or keep
virgin, the white fruit of winter's sky.

*

My mother was the true moon. Quietly
she sank through dark. Words do not hold their love;
they give back sudden, sharp to me
a scent I sometimes trust to be her own.
I am 'Arbelle' to Mary's quick French voice;
Grandmother's 'Arbell!' as a hound is called.
I am Arbella. If you think this voice
should beg or teach, forgive me – ghost:
look through our names. The glass is black,
the boy is dream's dark air; whose coldness blows
through me, finds me separate; strangely grown:
a prison filled with dogs and scratching monkeys,
red silk, and scraps of song, becomes my home.

Mary (of whom my grandmother held care),
my godmother, had married, till eyes hardened
that twisted boy my father's brother. Air
exploding gold, he fled the shaking house –

garrotted by her lover in a garden.
Mary drew blood. I watched her flare to power
tease with the old Earl, with tender eyes;
spit like a cat at her embroiderer's wife.
Then her chins were double, her hair dyed:
her voice was silk. She wound me in for life
poor trembling fish! Pity and charm, pale sun's light
crossing the clawed bedcover, she drew gently
inside her circle, worked: In my beginning
is my end. 'I do not understand,'
the young men flushed. She laughed. Did she?

Wisdom to her was emblems. She was Papist;
which even then, I feared. I loved cold light.
Canvases framing hearts and appletrees
diverted her, she claimed; impulsive, bright
she was a child, never fearing time
(her will bequeathed to me her Book of Hours)
but she feared pain, and new pain clawed her heart.
From her safe bed she gave me dusty sweets,
I coughed on sugared roses, as she told
how she had slept in Scotland on the moors,

wrapped in a plaid; woke there, the horses still
like stone; their live breath smoking; the great hills
melting in light, as in her chaplain's hand
the small, protecting cup shone ringed with gold.
I told my grandmother, half-doubting this.
She stared. 'She made some play to hold her rule
and much too late. She told me she had sewed
in Council; never listened-' There she stopped;
the room's vast dark her judgement: fool and fool.

Loud and short the final quarrel came:
Mary with her dogs and scrambled silk
banished. She did not say goodbye to me:
she died then; when they sent the gilded book
years on it hurt me, thinking her alive.
The circle ended. I could not begin.
In her scrubbed room I sniffed the dustless air,
The day was white with Derbyshire's cold spring.

'God be my judge, they dare not send her back!'
Now those eyes find my sleep. Then at our prayers
they read each text of vengeance until Hell
where Mary was, rose in their blaze of black.

*

They scolded my sharp tongue. I knew it came
from her; I would to God that it could cut
her picture from her frame, turn night to day
show you the kind of marvel that she was,
as beautiful as the great birds of prey
that ruffled in her mews. Where Mary sagged,
her skin grew taut, a white light lit her bones;
and so at forty-eight she caught her Earl.
She killed him too. She split each family
she married into, clawed them with contempt.
I will not list her marriages and beds,
her inventories do that. But I declare
all legends of her true, even her dying
(although I was not there).
Some fortune-teller told her she would live
until she ceased to build. She'd credit that,
though strong she looked for strength; burnt my hair-
    clippings

lest witches took them; had some private crafts
I know but cannot prove. The mortar froze.
The Chatsworth builders shrugged and turned for home.
She drove there in her carriage, raged at them,
for her cold eyes they heated cauldrons – nothing
could warm the frost. She saw the wall abandoned,
dragged home, and in the valued, dark bed died.
She was like the cold winds where she grew
her hating left mine feeble when it flared;
her stone initials raised to sky the only
emblem or human sign for which she cared.

II.   Interregnum

I am no emblem: and my name
is light
as pale silk or thistledown
too bright
for those who hold the signet and the seal.
Men weary of the old capricious Queen,
I come too late: their eyes look for a boy:
I make stiff-skirted curtsey to the Queen.
Her gold eyes flicker through me –
this royal glove, this toy –
for whom some perfumed closet is the place.

By boat we leave the slippery stairs. How far
the Queen's Thames swells in bursting tides of power,
too rough to hold my young and frightened face.

*

Our flowers were not as yours. You would not understand
how bluebells and small primroses shone warm
in our great gardens; they were all we had.
The flowers were gone with spring. Oh there were roses
pouring down each arbour and incline –
the damask and the musk
the briar and eglantine –
drenching us with sweetness till July
when they dropped brown and brittle. Freeze the spring:
our wisdom knew no second flowering.

*

Come dance with me, on gallery and stair,
my dance of idleness.
The dark spy codes: 'A lady shut in chambers
the English will not take into their hearts.'
I learn to sing (though with too thin a voice),
to sew with subtle thread,
to ride when storm and pestilence
allow me from the house: I learn the arts
of the noblewoman, or the small white dancing bear.

Also I learn Hebrew and speak Greek
and read the Bible daily without love.
I have one friend: my chamber's maid Jane Bradshaw
who combs my pale hair. At twenty-eight, lean moons,
the prisoned years close round me. You who are
stunted and chill, I stumble in your dance.
How painfully we lean to touch, how far
the great Thames swells – but that is not my tune.

III. Ghosts of Power

It is time to think upon New Year
to make the Queen a present for this time.
Derbyshire under rain pours blue and green
along the window in the gallery –
yes, light enough, Grandmother. I can see.
It is the high time of her final house;
Back we were carried, back where she was born;
in her new palace on a bitter ridge
like birds we huddle, shaken by the storm,
no Queen's at Hardwick; now she does not care
but measures the cream curving of her stairs
touches her tapestries. If dreams are grown
a prison, this is one, I hate each stone –
but in my hate, less power than Mary's had.

Here blow great hangings Mary never saw.
I tell her of them: 'Smouldered red brocade
has made a gown for tall Penelope.
She is not me. Although my eyes flash dark
she stares like Grandmother. Sometimes I see
your chestnut wildness in her. Gentle God
whose stern books I read coldly, let me free
out of these ghosts of power. This here is me:
Perseverance (worse worked); she is holding
a pale ungainly bird, that flaps to fly.'

In my hands flutters the uncrumpled lawn:
the Queen's white veil. Slow fingers, it is time
to edge with silver thread that hurts the hands
honeysuckle, trailing like a star
along the border; I draw tiny things
most curiously and well and without love.

I cannot walk into the villages – the pox is there;
hate me: I do not care,
my gentleness is folded in myself.

I have become the mistress of my dreams.
Grandmother watches less; I stay in bed
ignoring the dark morning; though it tugs
in my bed curtain and its yellow flowers.
Caterpillars curl along the frieze.
They shiver, gold. I close my eyes again.
Arbell, says the far voice, it is time –
I am Arbella and I walk with him
through a sea-city, light rings like a bell.
The morning is my kingdom. I am walking
among the children in a high salt air
(warmer than London's streets) and my long skirt
is lit with silver and disturbs no dust.
But his hand? I cannot hold it. Fading
as the gold air. I cough. The late wind whines.
Secrets fever me – hunched warm and close
above her veil, in the dark window seat,
reaching past a needle to a hand –
as though the cold air pricked me with its heat.

They bring in white candles to gentle the shadows.
My flourished veil is well-received. The Queen
sends a mean present but with kinder words
'would know how it is done'. I tell you, lady: keep
a soured nature in a winter house
as flowers drop silver, as the thin blood weeps.
So Mary's gifts were made. Sharp heart, laid to waste:
let this year spin me more than thread and sleep.

*

I had a cousin I had never seen:
I plucked grey quills, as snow falls, from the wing
of that ungainly bird my figure held –
          And many were the letters that I wrote.
I shudder now to feel them locked and lying
in a dry chest, their blots and wildness bare
for any eyes. For like a spare bright glove,
I set my cousin's name on my starved hand,
I wrote his guardian, asking we should meet –

I do not now recall I mentioned love.

The weather, strangely mild. The black mare was not mine.
Was she made hounds-meat with that willing mouth,
that quickening change of paces to my heel –
I would have buried her, for love. I must
call back that riding time: the hills a shimmer
in sheets of light, of silver and sharp black.
Dreams are as stuffs of dresses; you can feel
a quality where fingers brush. As wind
rushed my new life, I touched a roughness there:
too cold, too fixed. I struck the small warm flank,
along the hill's spine, galloped the black mare –
too fast, as the groom called. Words, horses, are
obedient, reckless; as those who ride.
Such sure feet did not fail. But all next day
the hills lay brown and sodden; almost silent
the Queen's men rode, sailors, on the mist's tide.

*

Do you still trust? Then never trust your kin:
my cousin sent my letter to his Queen.
I trust he had a fat purse for New Year.
To me, came Henry Brounker, a broad man
in brown-caked riding habit (foundering
through mud for days to check my misbehaving).
His greeting words creaked stiffly as a door.
Grandmother would have beat me if she could,
(her thin unloved granddaughter, turning wild),
assured him of her loyalty; she could,
being most loyal to herself. And I
left to the questioned air, cried like a child –
not at first, to them. But trust your kin.

I tested all the weapons of the weak;
I started with my mad self-pitying dream.
Imagined loves I twisted through my talk
and wrote at night strange, endless letters; streams
of words washed down my paper. Then as now
words were my country; then they failed me. How
can tears' heat see clear enough to write?
See true. It's hard. How sadly and how cold
I see my lit hair tangled in those nights
my blind hand scribbling, telling Brounker how
I loved the Earl of Essex – two years dead –
who had seemed to like me, as a child,
and when I spoke too loud, defended me.
(No wonder. He picked every losing cause:
a ready talent, which excuses me.)
At twenty-eight I should have looked beyond
those brilliant hazel eyes to policy.
But dead and lovely and my ally still
I summoned him: a ghost may write to ghosts,
as a slow girl retreats to thoughts of school.

But we forget too much: the murdering hosts
he could not check in Ireland; how he would
have rooted London up to snatch the Queen.
A word united us. The word was Fool.

I agree with good Erasmus: Folly
is a fine woman and she strips us bare.
Brounker spent hours noting answers, shaking
my branches, seeking treason's apples there.
'Who were your lovers?' he demanded. 'Names –'
The long flames flashed: I said 'My cousin James.'

He dropped his pen. The slobbered Scottish King!
His mouth hung open as the black ink spread.
I hissed triumphant. I was Queen and Eve
but mocking blew love's candles from my head
and left me on a cold-lit, lonely stage.
I loathed each scene and like a drug drew more.
Sent up the right stair from the Gallery
I entered, flaring, through the left-hand door.
They started, cold: a second, I had been
the royal phoenix, heiress of her blood.
What did Grandmother say; to shatter me?
And why did I return? Some word, some note? I could
sustain no noble act. My memory
melts tricks and scenes like snow, and finds beneath
a fevered mind, the impotence of rage –
the Queen's fox-red so briefly flamed my hair.
I turned the mirror. I had left the stage.

Then, as far lust and intrigue fell away
I clawed against the windows to be free.
I would not eat while I was in that house:
that was the sharpest gift they gave to me:

that I could die. Mary had lingered, fat.
My face grew hollow and I seemed to see
faces behind their own. I pushed away
the tainted chicken and the sugared pap.
And so I gained my only victory.
They let me leave Grandmother, carried me
to Wingfield, the old house where I lived
spoilt by grooms and tutors, as a child.
And such I felt, lying in the great bed,
as weak as after birth. Then as I learned
the old Queen died on cushions without sound –
night courtiers spurred to Scotland – the spring tide
rushed up the Thames, till round my sleep, it turned.

IV. The Court

Dark pendulum,
swinging time,
are you invented yet?
The centuries blur lightly.
The sharpest eyes forget.
But Court clocks chime.
Allow me to present
a true and most un-Christian
Testament.

I leave my best brocade
(white roses at its hem)
to the girl who vomits, after feast,
while courtiers cry 'Amen'.

Next best, my chastity,
I leave the Maid of Honour with red hair
(so recently returned to Court); or to
the wailing child left in a tenant's care.

I leave my thin waist to the heavy Queen.
Also my pregnant mind, to swell
in her, who made us sit upon the floor
to play at childish games. Since she was kind,
(grin not so, Death), I also wish her well.

I leave beside the nervous King, a dream:
a great moth which by moonlight bangs the pane
a window with no ready catch, that he
may hold no wretched soul at court again
lying of his love to them. But pause,
he dreams already (Death says) of worse things.
The moth is drowned in blood. Strike out that clause.

I leave my soured mouth and aching head
and my great debts, to hell,
which would suit courtiers well,
but not my servants; give them better days.

Observe that I do not bequeath my heart.
What lover's hand was cut
by the sharp tongue of art?
To you, I give the petalled truth of names.
So I, the noble Lady the King claims
'guid cousin' – and too fully in my mind,
leave all – except the Court of my lord James.

*

And yet I laughed, when first at Court,
innocent, at a Christmas play.
(My lodgings lie against the street
smudged with November, muddied grey.)
Far shines the young and shuttered hand
my sly and red-haired Chaplain took,
who called me lovely, learned, said –
my frail sixteen-year body shook –
if he could serve me, I must speak.
And while I trembled, fallen, bright
he was packed off, within a week.

Too near, my steward quietly
brings in black books for tallying.
'Sit down,' I say. But to my side
he stands, unadded; trembling
only when I turn suddenly,
caught by a blacker line: 'I see
the yellow pearls are pawned again.
You must redeem them next month for
the birthday masque.' (Young eyes fix dark,
Mine blur from focus.) Then the Queen's
plump birthday gift –

                    They think me poor
whose jewels and dress – as he contrives –
might feast a cottager for life.
Everyone I know has debts
they never pay. (Have I paid Hugh?)
My fine nose quivers. He has spun
some threadbare plan: a short-term loan.

Relieved, I praise. His cheek rots red.
So, dreamer, I am set for sale:

And you would save me? Yes, it would
be a warm, an easy bed;
Though ladies marry stewards, this
is mockery; a fairy-tale
of second-best, sad charity.

Carts rumble: a girl begs and calls
in high chill whining 'pity me,'
he shuts the thick door softly. That is all.
That earth could freeze...
                    The streets smell foul.

                    *

Cloud shadows drift the bank. On Hugh's old cloak
Jane and I count scratches; down hill paths
Hugh rode into the villages to seek
a carpenter. The coach leans where gorse burns;
stung gold, I see the axle snapped in half.
The groom's boy, whistling, trots each horse in turn
between the banks, through brown and dying may.
Such is my summer progress through these parts,
bumping the tracks, avoiding pedlars' carts;
stopping at will; but when our slow path crossed
Hardwick's glittered shadow. There breath paused.

The coach broke – first – soon after. I sent Jane
in a low shop where once they let me buy
ribbons for pearled dolls. Jane found a fine
red flannel. It would line our winter skirts,
the woman said, come out to me; her black
sharp eyes grew falsely tender as she cried
I had been gone too long – I should come back:
and Jane drop more true coin in her hand?

No, beggars are the debt we cannot lose:
warmed and sore, I watch a new group come,
their long coats patched with purple, like a bruise:

they set a child down and watch her keenly
clutch the wild, white roses they have sent,
constantly spilling petals in their spent
light glow: the white face of a gentle child.
Hers is hard brown. The clenching hand without
the roses needs a crutch. Slow as she comes
dispassionate sun lights on the hanging foot,
the long red scars. She halts, unsure
before the bank, the cloak; swings round to see.
They shout. Uncomprehending like a dog
she shivers, ducks and thrusts the flowers at me.

Do you dream I bought her, like a horse?
a child I could have touched but for a sense
she'd bite? Death clawed her where no words can soothe.
Uneasily I bend to her and ask
'who hurt your foot?' Not words but smells of alms
open this rose. Her sharp teeth shine. She smiles
'Dog got me, lady, up at Marchand's farm.'

Hardwick had dogs. The dark eyes flash five years
when I slept here, in winter's flowered bed;
Jane stares in warning but I hand the child
what my purse holds. She turns, black pupils flared,
small, hopping dust, she leaves as light as bird!
they will keep my money; she is spared
a beating till tomorrow: all I bought
of one day's sun. In light streets where Hugh calls
the son comes, the old man sleeps by damp walls
through fevered June the white dust drifts and falls.

Jane's brown eyes wonder what to say to me.
Beggars are vermin, though the child was lame.
If I sold all my jewels and won the King
I could buy land. I could live here again.
Nor Queen nor wife, half-fumbling, I would spread
warm in a quiet kingdom – much misled,
my wilful self denying, some slight good.

Kind dream. Far sun. Do your eyes give it home?
You know your clouds. I must describe my own.

*

Autumn was warm. I wondered; often fled
from fumes of court and from the golden air,
I pleaded a sick head
slipped Whitehall before supper. Then I wrote
quick as the light caressed me, to a friend
late gone from Court: who left me a white dress
gold with honeysuckle, peaches – unworn, but too voluptuous
too young – too rich to waste.
                                              'If any land
should be set for sale in our cold country,
I beg that you will let me know at once.
Concluding, Madam, your most loving friend.'

I do not sleep. I will survive a while:
in which I can bear London, hear the river
lapping the long houses, undecayed,
till my new dream, my garden is half-laid.
I plant its twisted paths with camomile
with thyme and rosemary; sharp scents there rise
from feet; sharp chaffinch cries; in hedges, closely twined
strength marries sweetness, hawthorn clasps rose briars.

Arbours, I train; set tables, deep in leaf.
If money grows I will fetch rareties,
fritillaries: great ruby butterflies
to thrust the snow (beside what hedges hold:
violets, that lend sleep; cowslips; the hazed
blue of forget-me-nots. I must confess
though I was trained in still-rooms, I was lazy
to learn of plants. Now I will raise my own).
With gilliflowers, the late pinks, I will try
to coax the North's late summer past July.
Diligent at evening I will look
through neighbour's herbals, legendary books
which mingle strange and sweet, and lie about them all.

Marigolds blaze in every half-kept yard
outside my gate; I'll not forget – The garden
lingers, unmade, into my sleep and claims
a dark elusive scent: a flower no herbal names.

V. Meetings

I hated fooling; round the windowseat
the bright heads gathered, teasing round his name;
though he was young from Cambridge, new to Court
what pricked me was my sharp dislike of them.

'Lady! sweet William will not speak with you,
he only reads.' My title's snow, sad power
to freeze. 'You gentlemen are ignorant:
such ignorance has named me too, a scholar.'

The face turned flushed. My glance lit on grey eyes;
then, as he bowed, indeed the student's bare
thin fingers. Something warmer crossed his face,
perhaps he did not see me but a dress:
spring's hem of white   gold throat of summer's fruit.
Still cold I watched the others drift from sight
dropped my name in a flattering drink of light
where black glass shone behind a draughty seat.

Mistrust such plays for power. Dangerous, distracting were
the dancers in far noise.   I kept aside,
the stiff skirt darker gold. We spoke of much.
His slow voice touched against the poets' Greek,
to me cold voices, cry of migrant birds
music too late for truth. I turned this speech
quickly to mock, cry dreamer. If he heard
it did not reach; he asked, light eyes assured,

'where shall our names live, lady; but in books?'

Not yours, I shook, not mine, the face
the glass held, trembling, bright,
into the dark where I felt frost gleam hard.
I rose. I saw his manners fall away:
the hand he reached to shrank like snow
sensing the Court's noise rising, tides of gold,
low, absurd I heard him say
I had saved him; I was his 'gracious moon':
that he would ride and thank me in bright day.

Alone, too quickly I let fall the dress.
There was an ink-stain half-scrubbed on the hand
I took too lightly. I must face him soon,
I who thought love dignified and kind, stand:

with ten years fading, scuff the dress –
gold dancer, bare feet tingling, sudden dark
dissolving every sense in foolishness,
mistrust the shows of power.
All that sustain me are
the roses on my skirt

Roses of air and fire

*

This is the letter I shall write to you,
between the candle's smoking and cold dew.

my dark dove and my dear
I fear you are too young
that for you light springs
in all you look upon.
Although I smile and tell you lies,
come close, there is old darkness in my eyes.

In spite I turn all mirrors to the wall
and watch myself swim small into your eyes,
lost in your depth of light you cannot know
there is a burning coldness makes me wise.
I beckon you, dressed in my borrowed flame
my masquing gown, you trot towards the snare,
I would cry to save you, you would leap –
but it is winter and the tracks are bare
and give no cover or escape but draw
slowly to my forest's dark
my dear

– who held his hand out to this fire. Lest
you see – conceit I give the coals. But bright
it fills the glasses' fingered emptiness
sharp, tender, blue: spring crocus tricked by light.

*

This fugitive and winter love
silvers the lips to frost. I wake, and shine.
The lean trees have no sap to write of us
– nor any rag of leaf, that we may hide.

Bare twigs beat at our faces as we walk.
Jane lingers after like a plump, dark, bird.
Wind pulls my hair loose from the golden pins,
and snatches all our speech, but for a word.

I dare not write. One frozen afternoon –
cold birds – we huddled on the draughty floor.
You kissed my throat in firelight. The logs flowered.
Jasmine, clear yellow for the winter sun
burned on the sills. In darkness, half unsure,
the wind's dogs scratch the thick transparent door.

*

Am I unkind? Before the Council, I
answered all, admitted nothing. They
might know with Brounker, I had cracked to glass,
but that was in a younger, fainter day.
Now on my unpaid gown and upright chair
the window's light was hardening. I sat cold.
When they informed me he had bought
their peace with tears; and a declaration

he would not treat of love with me again;
unshocked I told them 'I am sorry for it'
would not blur sight through tears, as women should.

Pity is not softness. Cold I wrote
reminding what he owed –
I knew that I could break him if he came.
I did not accuse but waited till
(shocked from out his books into my arms)
he cried, that he had given them his name.
I stroked the fine hair slowly; love: it's hard
to be strong to them who always come
too early, wake us shaking at a time
too unexpected, young;
when we are tender, and their cold eyes kind.

VI. Marriage

2 a.m.

The good die now, this cold clasped to their heart.
If human faces watch, they do not see.
Into death's dark I marry; yes, in part
as she my dead grandmother would have done
to suit my horoscope. The blacker art:
by dawn the ruffling birds will whistle, see
Jane and Hugh; the slow priest in whose church
we planned this (may the old cruel God forgive).

Candles blow breaths of cold. The new ring burns
gilt on my tender skin. Still cruel? to live

touch Jane's chill cheek, and strangely, Hugh,
leaning miles, trailing light; to keep
your quick cold hand in mine. Your scared eyes glow:

the black wicks smoke, we part, too late for sleep.

*

Such grace, your clumsy fingers made:
your gentleness held even when we failed,
and laughed, for reason that the night has kept;
that fumbled, likely bed, let your eyes close;
your hand smoothed on my small breast, and you slept.

Half-choked beneath the tightness and the fear
yet body opens generous as flame.
I dream, circled in fire: I am here
light with nowhere. Light becomes your name.

By falling coals we scrambled for your clothes,
I pulled the white shirt over your slow head,
I rubbed my hands against you till you warmed.
You spoke me in a new voice sleep had thickened
and left me, in the dawn, my vacant bed.

I walked between the beech trees' silver flesh.
Blunt ash buds stroked the sky. The Court and park
hung secret as the face your hands have framed.
The night you did not come, I slept; exposed
in dream, you hammered, building us an ark:

I said, 'He will not save us though he could'
(the constant knocking at the house door rose)
Where are you? So. Since no man drowns in tears

and since He does not kill and it is known
(my door is next) love's naked, wrecked in dark –

Dress quick. It is still cold. The high seas spurn
the wicked; leave them clothes and life alone.

*

That I knew you so briefly, now I grieve:
that I cannot remember, as I ought,
between cupped hands, a flame: that jerks sideways
and stings my wrist and yet remains
as luminous and tender as you were.

Do you still read? They have you in the Tower
whose cold invades the heart, as Raleigh knows
whose son has died for him in El Dorado.
I did not want your pain; not that hard power.

Yes, the good Bishop is my warder still.
I hope Hell has him. I admit I made
our journey out of London misery.
I screamed and took to bed. He was delayed,
ruffled from his wine, by such raw pain.
I did not have to act. Does dignity
still weigh with you? You are more dear to me.
Forgive. That's what he preached. Humility
obedience. How wicked, love, to grow
so wild, to weep. They carried me outdoors.
And now we are in Durham where the snow

is warmer than the wind – I never knew
such cold existed, till this northern world.
The town is small, the winds enormous. Hugh

brought a half-frozen bird down from the sill:
once fed it scrambled back into the storm.
(The people here speak lilting, strangely, Will,
their voices rise like birds.) Here you keep warm
and that is all. I will not see his Grace –
forgive; I am not sourer; I am warm
with Jane, and grow, to creatures, strangely kind.
I eat no meat. We live like creatures, here,
driven to draughty holes. Now I would like
some cat, some dog, to breathe upon my bed
but would not prison them. How Mary kept
monkeys; I told you that?

I will not say
I wished for months that I had borne your child
(though in a week from when they came, I knew)
and yet there is that vein of coldness in me –
the suckling done, would she have plagued me? Well
I keep no monkeys. And I will not say
still dazzled after sleep, I reach for you.

Your letters worry me. Have you been ill?
Can you see trees? Sunlight is hard here, clear
in ice-edged branches at the river's edge
held out of the flow. I feel you changed;
dreams should not freeze as I am frozen here.

I end in hope. His Grace leaves word: the King,
now I am quiet within my cage, may let me
like some unnatural bird, go South for spring.
I send you flowers, though they are Durham's snow,
furring the sill, upon the blue glass, thickening.

VII. Escape

'Think,' I urge, 'when you were newly married,
if you had been kept from him for so long – '
Her hand puts down the apple it has peeled.
She smiles at me, this soft and fair-haired woman:
lady of a house so lightly guarded.

I am glad your letters turn more tender –
or could I cheat her so? Let my eyes close:
I see my worn face bent to kiss your shoulder.
Through fire's kind heat, I shiver. (I have been ill.) 'You know
it is arranged; but for one night alone.'

The apple peelings, delicate, flush brown.
Her warm face is left shining by my lies.
Look in the books, good dreamer, for her name
which I have forgotten. With no shame –
I honour still the kindness of those eyes.

I wear, for her, the full set of men's clothes:
soft boots, the muffling cloak, the swaggered sword.
She laughs until she chokes: a trick I use,
a glancing humour: as a mirror whirled
comes back with all the world behind your head.
She pours me wine. The ceiling flashes swords –
finished, I plant upon a chair, astride.
Passing me the glass, her fingers shake,
as do my own. For I am terrified.

*

In the wet yard, the lantern wavering,
they brought another horse. I only wished
a friendly ditch: to lie, until the ache
left me and the noise of horses died.
Raw brandy dazzles eyes. The groom's boy, opening
a yellow space of kind light blurred by straw,
turned the tired horse to watch them heave me on.
I heard him tell the groom across the door
'That gentleman will not hold out to London.'

Before you see the road or smell the fight,
that voice says 'you will not –' and fades to night.
I cannot hold this horse, unschooled and pulling strong.
I have not ridden all the prisoned year,
I never rode astride. My soft thighs run
into a childish quivering of pain –
as pot-holes drop, again, again I'm thrown
at the sharp pommel; or I snatch the mane.
The rattling riders call, but dare not use my name,
I do not speak; as if my silence would
drown out their rough feet on flint and mud,
their pace that aches my arms and numbs my blood.
I scarce see low Orion; the snatching trees; my hands
translucent from the sickness, burn with cold
in clumsy gloves, claw back the dangerous rein.

Out of the jolting dark, words beat my head
to drive back the boy's whisper in the yard,
not gentleman – hold out to London – will not –
cold heart, as tired legs stumble, I rise jarred,
my body, urgent in its pain, knows what
the worn hoofs beat: that harmony is hard.

*

where the black river-waters hissed
they pulled me down, I looked for you:
strained through the dark, I would have kissed
your cold mouth there for ever, but they said
you were delayed; climb in the boat.

I drifted fevered, stupid love.
(The boatman stared at my white hand,
drawn fretful from a man's hot glove.)
Dimmed moon in fog, our ship's light dipped.
(Come late, you found another ship.)
The fog had filled our minds. All captains plead
the turn of tide: too weakly, I agreed.

Slowly, we entered on the open sea.
Enormous waste. I leaned against the rail
in a dark, strange gown Hugh had for me.
I rode the tilting till my sickness died.
I spoke to no one. All I heard
was sea; or from the rigging in black sky
men cried, incomprehensible and high
till my thoughts turned and made another world.

Dawn was icy, tender. Calais lay
a smudge at our eyes' edge. Hugh ran to say
when we would land: a stranger, smiling there.
I did not use his name. 'Find me the captain, say
my plans are altered. We will anchor here.'

I thought that he would strike me. I stared back
the unused power: the great eyes blazing black;
the voice blew dawn's blank air. 'We wait for him.'
He shouted in the wind. I turned about
gripping the splintered rail, stiff and salt.

Out of low mist the gold ship rose and fired –
smoke settled low in sun. The sailors cried
gulls whirled – the voices plead. We are surrendered.
They climbed on board. Their eyes turned to a wild
creature of their mind. I only said
'Did you take him?' then 'I am thankful for it.'

They bowed to me. Exemplary and grand
the mistook tide broke over all we planned.

*

He was not cornered in the chartered ship.
He was in Holland; gales had blown him there.
My grandmother laughed from some wicked place;
she would have been in Calais, counting sheets.
Mary would have lingered some time there
staring at the sun; until, despair
worked out, she would seek Paris from the port,
to close her fine dark circle in the Court.

Absurd. I wept for days. Slowly I came to see
what might have waited us: the muddy inns;
a woman with bright name but all looks faded.
More brutally, I might have swelled
to meet the septic knife in childbed.

He was my love; but I had played him coldly.
Had he been less young, the howling air
not swept them down the coast, I do believe
he would have turned from land and waited there.
I could not risk them taking him again;
be gracious as the moon,
confirm I paid that debt.
Hard as the rail's wood, my memory
escapes me and the emptied hands forget

all but the barren air to which I came.

VIII. The Tower

Old tapestry, blown green, like summer leaves
in dreary kindness narrowed more the room.
A high small window let the North light beat
but day died soon; I used to walk
upon the battlements; they rose as cold
as wind on Hardwick's roof; at other times
I walked beside the warder's crusted walls.

God whom I only name, in outer air
the lanes are rushed with light of great spring rains;
white tails of sheep's-wool drip among the briars
moss glitters on the sun's untrodden stone.

Love, your face is gone, in a far air.
I do not think the king will let me free,
I am that risk no State will dare.

Kin crumbles, I remain. This room holds me
not for a day but years of boredom, cold.
Cut in a wall not far from here:
my father's name. I carve no such remains.
A braver woman or a saint might kneel;
in twenty years, James' son may pardon me
what's left; the Court sniffs 'mad', short spring
revives the free, damp eats my body old.

Starvation's not a death I recommend.
At times I float and watch strange colours flow
free as you are; and still more free
could I dissolve – Death's horrible. I burn
and choke on dregs of food. Physicians say
that something else is there; would God grow kind?
Kindness I fear most of all, would keep
Jane from me with her endless steam of soup,
beasts' blood. Now I trust Hugh (who planned escape
when first I came, then married, suddenly).
He wraps the pearls (their gold glow soft and deep)
part to pay them, part to buy drugs, for me,

so moons melt black; buy dear, short sleep.

*

Truth must be quick. It may not grieve
that wakeful silent air,
by retching death, post-mortem, more
of body's history – you would not want this.
Say I grew light, take from my sleep
the warm quick pulse by which you live

which beats through time and power
(the tides of language burn)
a word of snow the moon's light
in bitter grace consumes.

Say it was not your eyes I kissed,
say words grow light, and listening cold,
such love beats in this unnamed dust
towards that dreaming power you hold,
stirring, I warn, we wake and must
break cold from dream find life the ghost.

*

But bitter dust: to write in Mary's book
'your most wretched Arbella' with your name,
and send it you that you might suffer too.
(It is preserved in Russia; do they see
a sumptuous fossil, her silk circle; or,
beneath the glass, the trembled script of pain?)
My dreams still saw you in the window seat –
but holding you, a tall girl with dark eyes –
I was not tall; what longing might reach you?
Yet pain grows lighter, yet I will declare –
I who dreamed you brave when you were young,
that I saw in you truly what you were:
that all men praised you in the civil war
and that your second marriage, the safe bed,
accounts and the deep orchard, could not shut
those clear eyes I had kissed, to misery.
You called your tallest daughter Arabella:

my light name in her, something grew from me.
I ask that girl who walked her mother's orchards,
picked blossom, white unprofitable flower,

had you not realised I was ordinary?
The woman late from work who washed her floor
the man who leaned against the whitewashed wall
stared at the work's black door;
I could not reach to grasp the reins of power;
beside, the horse was bolting; not the strength
but weakness of my cousin's son plunged England
to fighting in white orchards and wet moors.
The age of Queens was over. And my garden
flowers slowly and with ever lower walls;
do you see each man valuable and loved
or truly answer to a common name?
my own faults make me tremble; my mistakes
cry first against me. Only risks are proved.

And our own power known last: the years the cold house closed
unkind and stunted. Still to me
most simple and most strange to understand
Is that we do not reach. As I lost you.
Light fills the winter branches, the great sun
beats against the glass and we are there
frozen in love. And love I briefly am
to cry to you in a cold name we pass
as light into bright air and endlessly −

but I died cold: a new pain tore my heart
and none of this at all could comfort me
or wake me as the tide bore down the Thames,
death's flood lets no voice or lover through
strips down the tapestry –
spring's moons explore
the flowers of ice, clear glass,
touch light: wake you.

The Birds

I come back to the students' shabby cloakroom,
To listen to the birds. Their nest is out of sight;
Leaning from windows, in the cool, comes near
Their high dusk crying. Sparrows? no, too sweet.
Starlings? I would not think so. Swallows, yes.
I watch the brown hill shrink. I hear
Sea in their voices, continents of heat.

Rented Rooms

Night stole away my reason to be there –
that routine note which missed the post. I came
out of the throaty mist, the New Year's air,
stared, at the dim house which showed no name,
called to a girl, who rattled past her bike,
blowing her fog-damp scarf, winter's hot cheeks.

The first door I pushed open from their hall
gaped a conservatory, shadowed: full
of spoiled ferns once, sweet geraniums.
Now it held bikes, askew. It breathed back all
the cold of first streets, lingering on stairs –
the outside door blows open – no one cares
to clean: from Christmas, ivy curls in sprays,
dark, in rolls of dirt. Who went away
leaving this television blank above
a rolled-up quilt? Quick: drop the printed note
on the hall's floor.

                        It echoes back again
the deep sea chill of fog, the waves of dust,
my wonder at a room's dimmed lights.
Need, then:
the stairs to silence; not to own, but love

Whose Window?

Whose window are you gazing through,
Whose face is stilled between your hands?
The glass glows deeper than your eyes
Where quick lights sink: as feet through sands.

Into your darkness first snow drives,
No soft meander, aimless drift,
But straight as water. Crumbling bright,
Sharp crystals flash, as if they lived.

Now when the great wind throbs the door
When street-light and small hedge are drowned
My face turns open into night.
I am not safe. No, I am found
Melting the hard bolts back. The hall
Is filled with dark air, ice-clouds blow:

A warm face sleeps. I am the snow,
Uncatch your window. Let me through.

Half-day

Padding the green alleys of my grass
Watching jackdaws crest upon the roof
I sit, red dock seed rustling by my head.
Great hollyhocks sway up from last year's roots.

My neighbour's child cries, her mother shouts
'I'm busy with the ironing! You must come in or out!'

So she goes in. And it is sad, the quiet,
The grass still warm, seed-silver. Will she lift
Her face from cloth's slow steam: will she find out
Ironing is duty; summer is a gift?

Apple Country

I am living, quite unplanned, by apple country.
Worcesters come the earliest: sea-green
With darkest red, even the flesh, veined pink.
They have a bloom no hand can brush away
Sweet breath made visible. But do not think
To have them through the dark days: they'll not keep.
For that, choose Coxes flecked with gold
Which wrinkle into kindness, winter's fires.

Where I was born, they let no flowering trees
In the bare fields, which grow my dreams, which hold
Only the lasting crops: potato, wheat.
How low the houses crouch upon their soil
With fruitless hedges; at the barn's end, cars:

None yours. I have no art for probing back
To such dark roots. Yet if you pass this place
Though skies shine lean with frost, no softness dapples
White wall to cave of leaf, yet, stranger, knock

For I will give you apples.

Monday

The air was dark with rain, the day
Held little promise. And I stared
At all the bills, the things to do:
Then I saw you there
At the dull page, in the lamp's glare.

I laughed. Love is not easy, cannot
Will us one or win us time.
Weeks fray us open like a knot.
Worn: all separate: we shine.

Medine in Turkey

'Today' said Hassan – through a mouthful of honey –
'A girl will come who speaks French.' There came
A girl with straight brown hair, her eyes
Flecked with gold, a stiller honey.
Her French was pure and soft. Her name
Was Medine. Her paid study
Ended when her father died.
'Maintenant – j'aide ma mère. Je lis.'

'Je lis Freud,' she ventured, bare feet firm
On the rug's blurred leaves. She lived next door.
Each house leads to a tiny yard
With a dusty tree; white chickens squirm
In favourite hollows. She never saw
France; she sat, this grave brown child
Ten years younger than myself, unmarried
Alight, in their cool best room. She smiled.

There is no answer. Scholarships?
France, too, has hot bored villages
With girls who read all afternoon.
The arranged husband, or their child's care
Will not close up that watchful face
Flecked by lace curtains, endless sun;
Unmoved, she listens for the place
Where the book closes, where the footsteps run.

Bookkeeping

These are not (you understand) the figures
which send cold judgement into the backbone
which leave us, workless, shrunk at home
staring in a sky grown black with leaves.
These are like the ticking of a clock,

the daily sums, a van's new brakes,
three drums of trichloroethylene on the back
of a thrumming lorry; yet they take
a day to make: thin bars of figures. While
I try to balance them, light scurries round
like a glad squirrel. Radio music stales –
until shut off.

        What's left when it is done,
the green book closed? There is no sea to swim
no mouth to kiss. Even the light is gone.
Bookkeepers drink over-sugared tea
lie in dark rooms; are always hunched and tired.

Where I stretch up the low bulb burns and whirls.
And in it, I see him. The dusky gold wing folds
across his face. The feathers' sharp tips smudge
his margins.

Sunk, in his own shadows, deep
in scattered ledgers of our petty sins:
he, the tireless angel:
Unaccountably, he sleeps.

Last Week

Last week I had two rows with my superior,
my best friend chose to leave. There was a bomb scare:
we shivered for an hour, among clouds of smoke and daisies
(the smoke was cigarettes, they found no bomb).
I promised next, to strike, risking the dull future –
not the best of weeks, in short. Again, the lilac
hangs heavy over other people's fences
and when no one is looking, after rain
I draw the sprays close to me, breathing slower,
brush from my face the cold and vivid water.
The martins have returned, from unimagined seas'
wind-blinded miles, as sudden as they left,
their bow of wings, stubbed tails, boldly black
wheel and turn above the crumbling flats;
how tall they make the houses look. The sky
stays further than I thought, further and higher.

Homecoming

Horses have quick routes they know
A few safe roads, down which they always go,
They are not tempted by the sudden lane
The silver poplar shivering in light.
They only crave heaped hay again,
And pull to keep the low white yard in sight.

So I must fight them, if I am to go
On fruitless roads, on past the dulling tree;
Nor could I tell them, even if I knew
What it was we turned so far to see,
Before the hungry stables of the night.

Hill Mist

I am too fond of mist, which is blind
without tenderness; whose cold clings close
round the face.

The timid horse likes it;
treading his own space,
he cannot see black haystacks loom
the dog wait in wet woods; the man
crouch in brambles, raise a gun,

Even its sound is muffled. Death would be quiet in the mist.

Up on the crest – though you will say
he bucks, he gallops – how calm you seem
rising soundlessly over the grass.

Mist lets you in – All I see are the dancing
lights advance: evaporate.

The mist grows into a strange horse
the slender chestnut mare – the solid man, we saw
once riding with a woman; always, now, alone.
You make as much of this as the white shapes
smoke, in my eyes – All I will say
is, he is hard, as ground is: in bravado
rides bareheaded. How the mist must cling
to him. As you step out, our horse's mane
hangs heavy, dewed and glinting.

There is no past here. The only future's
The hidden gallop's heat. It is a place
I did not mean to love. Do you live so:
Walking your own space?

Grooming

Mud hangs its dried beads on your eyelid,
Not on red and glossy hair, but the dark skin
Too tender to be brushed. I hesitate
And then I lick the sponge and touch it to you.
You sigh with pleasure, slip your heavy head
Into my other hand: and let me rub.
Stepping round, stroking your ears, I think
We are too narrow, and our labels
Far too few.
All the loves and all the warmth shut out –
The yard is empty. Finished, like this horse
Who on the hill-top cries for his own kind –
How suddenly, intensely, I want you.

Mr Street

He praised your shoeing, then your ease
In riding; said, as you were seventy-three,
That you were selling all the horses up.

Gone: as stars scatter. Now I see
Why you worked so hard on me, to buy
Martha, half Irish drayhorse, who would stand
By shuddering buses like a rock; and my
Beloved Joshua; dark, springing horse
With fine and ruined legs. You even tried
Tall Brandy, who could buck me to the sky,
But had him safely sold to someone else.

You were a rescuer. The wilful mare
Who, because a bit had chipped her teeth
Fought every bridle, let you slide hers on.
You had a stout brown pony, thirty then,
Whom you 'kept meaning to put down', but always
Went on; and on. The pied New Forest pony
Hobbled your paddock upon swollen feet
You daubed with healing tar. Who will buy them?

But it is true, the work was heavy. I
Remember as you led them for a ride
After the catching, shoeing, grooming – what
Strange sweat lay on your brow: like a sharp dew
Silvered: a warning. So you heard at last
Your heart's complaint, to outlive horses. Yours

I've heard you number, like a liturgy,
Jumbo, Candy, Pepper, Topper, Patch –
You talked fast as you rode. Can your yard be
Empty? Is your house dark? They have not
Gone. They stand, behind your shoulder. See.

from Breaking Ground

a conversation with John Clare (1793–1864),
farm labourer and poet, who died in an asylum

On the Boards (spoken by John Clare)

I turned a boxer: although short,
With my great drive to the jaw
Each time I fought I laid my man
Cold, on the bare white board.

So I grew known at country fairs:
And all the boys ran after me,
Young women raised their children high
That they might turn, and see.

Then dukes and earls paid all my fare
That I might go to London,
But where I left the warm coach there
I saw a sky made stone.

In high lit rooms, I drank white wine
Which let my tongue strike quick,
Cut glass rang stars, deep carpets lay
Red as my blood and thick;

But when I came back late that night,
All rooms were dark, none home.
No man I knew in all those miles
To give me bread or room

Then I walked home: and lost three fights:
And was despised by men
Who fed me porridge and raw meat
To have me fight again.

But He, with eyes remote as stars,
Reared up to twice my size
With one great blow, He split my head
And so I sank and died.

The village shutters closed at noon.
The children, with bare feet,
To the crying of my bell
Ran out along the street

And filled the church and stood in rows
To watch the coffin pass
And on the bare and boarded box
Cast every flower there was,

Marigolds of sun and flame
Light stocks as sweet as women's love
Briar roses, frail as wrists of girls,
With every thorn plucked off –

Because I faced the sun for them
And cast the dark shapes down
Still they will sing me, warm and free,
Though I am locked in ground.

Enclosure

Look down –
you ride the cold air, as he dreamed,
but cannot rise so far
as the white mounds of cloud-floor, the high and breathless air;
that blue he dreamed: not saw.
Chill trails, low mist part round you. Peer and see
a moor; a waste; stretches of green and grey
marked by faint tracks, rough slopes where great trees stand;
small cattle, like dark grain, watched by a boy
or an old man – no hedge, wide road to break
this land of mist, space: silence. It is England
unenclosed. That space was never ploughed.
Slow in the uncut grass my skirt sweeps dark,
my feet start up deep dew. Fresh mushrooms here
burst warm: as white as flesh. Did it once seem
the fields were mine?

                              'I drove sharp furrows miles,
till waves of mud upon my strong boots weighed
and clogged me: but on land we worked each year.
The commons' grass was greener, tense with time,
with flowers you could not now dream: the brief
orchids' dew-white, glistening mouths. I knew
each sheltered tree; their deep roots bound my life.
To see that free land broken by the plough:
it was as though men cut my body through.'

'There was a time when every elm tree died,
not in one place, but thousands. They were burned –
People took fear at it; as though the fire
which crumbled bark to ash, marked their own end.

Is there no strength in us: to ride, past change?
England lay forest once – '

'You speak too narrowly.
You speak like them.'

                    He kicks a rotting stump,
woodlice shower from it, over lumps
of creamy wood: they scramble, to get free.

'Think what you saw: the cattle, sent to feed.
Whose were those pastures? They were common land;
all he had, that herd-boy, running down
behind a milk-cow, stamping at the cold.
The tracks lay anyone's. You walked all day
and never saw a fence. But part by part
the wild ground was divided; shut away
hedged by its owners' shadows: a rich land, without heart.'

I think of building-sites, how fires glow good
and warmth to winter. With the builder gone
dark, woven fences, ruffed gold flowers in rows
which are not let to mix or seed
 Enclose. Enclose.
He picks white bramble-flowers clustered low,
one pink – to twist them through a buttonhole.
The fruit glints black, looks sour. From frost, so soon?
He lopes, half-gipsy. Would he understand
deep towns or us: shut in them, patiently?
His light is open land.

'How is your county?'

'Rich,' I say, 'well-drained,

The fields are huge: skies sweep them, stunt them; now
nó drifts of cowslips as my father found,
their throats splashed red; the sows live penned, inside.'

'And the enclosure –'

Once I drew its map
a child's crayon fields; remember, squelching black
unkind fruit; frosted: nothing sweet but seeds.
'The Earl of Scarborough built a carriage road –
whose cost, with hedging, fell upon all those
with any land; the poorer people sold
their ground to pay the debt. How much they owned
I cannot tell you; for they walked its measure
in strides too small for sense now: "perches", "rods" – '

'What I arraign is not the broken mist.
We had illusions, better without them:
perhaps – Nor will I halt and name again
the plants, the paths I loved, which they destroyed.
Listen; leave that fruit. Those men did this
with shut and unkind hearts, and for their own.
What happened to those people of your village
who sold ground to meet the Earl of Scarborough's claims?
I know your cities. They are fortresses.
They shut out light and care. Round all of us
there is a poorer world than England was
your open world – Behind your painted doors
you hide: and all you spare falls less,
than scraps we fed to pigs. Unclosed as day
my torn mind blows and shifts till I forgot

if you own God? Name one: so you may say,

he pardons you. I have none. I do not.'

Crewe to Manchester: December

When I was here last, foxgloves foamed the banks,
moon-daisies were dipping. I repeat this:
I cannot believe it. All I can see
is brambles' dark smouldering, quelled by the rain.

Where is the skewbald pony who wandered
field ridges in sunlight? The cattle seek high ground,
small ponds sweep in flood. It was a wild night –
Even the angler tramps back over fields,
his stream's swell too high to be borne.

Why did I wake
at three in the morning
wholly convinced it was dawn?

On the Move

They made no sound, then very close
came a rush, like wind. 'Jump on the gate!'
the old man called. The boy stared down.
They poured below, a sea of rats,
still made no sound, no twittering,
as starlings who in their high clouds
darken snow-fields. Purposely,
ignoring men, the rats swept on.

So said the boy, the truthful man,
my grandfather. I know no one
alive who saw such things. Then say
the rats belong to hungry time.
Today, below December's sun
wind whistled through an elder bush.
My skin crept tense. I heard the rush:
saw, on a bare road, two rats run.

One fled, a foot long, but its mate
smaller, turned on the broken verge.
The stacks held bait. Perhaps too late
or in their cool and perfect wit
to seek another shelter out,
they vanished through an open gate.

Where is our hunger? All you see
are corn-filled barns, for miles around.
Beside the broken elder bush
listen: though you hear no sound.

Hawthorn

May stinks. Why do we like it so?
For rust of buds, as last snow strikes at hills,
For freckled, open white which spills
Down dull lanes, shines to clouded skies.
Because it is early summer. So
The season I married, ten years ago
I walked through a town I longed to leave
Down by the river; heard evening breathe,
The swallows swish low. Now, I thought
All things may happen, from this day:
I was right, oh and wrong, sweet stink of the may.

Black Dog

Cold broods over the house, like a white stare.
Across the lamps' light, snow sprays feathers – stars –
You grind your blue shoes in my lap
All your new books are read.
                                    But there are stories
Which drift, before we sleep, as far away
As lonely barns, from which the crumbled straw
Spills snow on frozen ground. Here is a story
Without a start or end, from the flat land
From which I came.
                              Now, listen – You love dogs
The lumbering St Bernard, prancing Cairn –
A man is walking up a clouded lane
Head hot with drink; the night. What makes him turn?
High as the hedge, it stands. It watches him.
Its eyes are vast as stars.
                                    On the low road
Skimming the dips, the new, fast cycle runs.
Why does the rider brake? He hears its breath, behind,
He races on; the blurring wheels gleam.
Harshly it blows, yet it lopes after him
Past every elm and gate, mile after mile.

Then, when he rushes in, no longer hot
With clear, scared eyes, they listen; then they nod.
Almost amused, they tell him, what he saw
Was the Black Dog.
                              It is seen everywhere:
But where I started, grew the calm idea
That under berried hedges, padding dark
It comes to keep you safe: to friend the night.

So much quick time lies wasted. So much fear –
Of wind, that cuts you, that could light you through,
Of quiet spiders spinning in the sun,
Of dark. There as he looked (though it was gone)
Over the plaited hawthorn reared the moon,
Lifted, through threads of cloud, a beating light.

You wriggle to the floor. Older than you
Stories do not stay still. They melt, like snow,
Trickle through books, to shine along my shelf.
In times of thaw, wandering inside or out,
You may meet blacker dogs inside yourself.

The Horse Stops

Why do you look back so intently
Over the closed gate, up the lane
As if the January night were endless
As if you would never leave again?

Look, there is light. But the warmth is slipping
Over the land's rim, where the sun
Darkens the valley with gold and murex,
Flying blind to everyone.

'I'll come, tomorrow.' Yet you stare.
Your face as still and sharp as frost
Shifts into the light's ebb where
It finds, like breath, all that is lost.

Produce of Cyprus

Picking grapes from a paper bag, sucking the misted skin
I think of the island which grew them, Venus' ground
(the rain is in sheets on my window, wet, green, blind)
there, the dry song of the cicada, there the warm nights
with the window propped open, sea's stripe on the counterpane.

Yet they too, have their troubles. The frosts were late;
the land does not love us, relentless stony ground
though we own it down generations. The price of grapes
is falling; and so on. No doubt they dream of us
that far and prosperous country; on its window, the wealth of
    the rain.

The last is tough. The bag, as I put by the rest
rustles and whispers, Paradise is the place
of which we know nothing, which we know best.

School Dinners

Why do I dream now, of people from school?
I am not old. They are not dead.
Yet warm before waking they surface, thin,
or in Janice' case, still fat.
                                    She dyed her hair
in red rat's tails; thought brash. She hitched her skirt,
her wide thighs wobbled. She was kind as silk.
One day, chattering, tipped salad cream
over her favourite pudding;
                                    did remember
to ask the boy's address, but found it false.
They left the seaside camp. She had a daughter,

who now, I think, would be the age
of Janice in my dream; when giggling still
she reached out for the cheap gold-coloured jug.

Eight people made that table. Who do I still know?
No one who could tell me how she lives,
cooking vast Sunday dinners? married? happy?
My ignorance stays perfect as the moon
dropped, like a coin through a barley field,
drowned, in all the blue waste of the sky.

Sitting by my daughter in a car
borne smooth and cool, through tunnelled trees
it strikes me, quick as shivering, that when
they must end, yet I will see them there
small and clear, in the battered jug,
their mistakes; their tails of red hair.

Spinner

The spider walks across the air
He curls a long foot round his thread
His legs, brown-striped in sunlit grass
Jerk, as wakened from the dead.

So I; at last released from work
Can sit beside the unwashed glass,
See the slow spider stalk through space
Until a green half-hour has passed.

Then, as he twists and firms the thread
There swerves in me this sudden joy
Although his lightness turns a trap
Though all he makes there, will destroy.

Moths

Out of the dark the moths come, beating
Against ungiving plaster, waiting
Folded in our breathing rooms.
As they stay – quivered – you may look
To match their patterns to a book:
The scarlet thread, soft black in thumbs.
Though by next morning they have gone
Still they are clear, remembered, tame,
While, pale and sudden, new wings come
Whirl from the glass, and leave no name.

Woken

They have cut the tops off the grass.
The prisoners say, the seed
Will return its airy head
And plant the world.

Sometimes the prisoners see
Not awake – turning –
A face which passes for a moon:
A woman burning.

There are no prisoners here.
Some time in the night
There was a hand which found my face,
Careless as you, as light.

Collection

I have been round the bungalows again.
I hate them like the shaking grip of flu.
Even their lawns are shaved too close
with white and broken grass. Their earth holds rows
of parched bright marigolds a daughter came
to thrust in hurriedly one afternoon.
Then the rich groundsel sprang no back could bend
to pluck – No, in my hurry I confuse
the formidably neat, who still wear hats
skewered on straight; the wild, who slam their doors,
who talk to no one but those 'relatives'
who hold keys which, reluctantly, they use.

Halls smell of hot dust on electric air,
of one continual fire; of old paint,
a ghost of cabbage or of liquorice.
I edge from the glass door when shapes appear
I wave my envelopes and try to smile.
Do I rob them? Not all the old are poor,
some keep long cars, curtains in glinting folds.
My daughter in her vivid pink coat sleeps.
Unhelpfully, the round is for 'the old'.

Next year, I swear, I won't go back again.
My feet are burned by steps. My eyes are sad
from all that dull paint. Yes, I am afraid
not of the feebleness that is the old –
the slack wrists – but their fierceness, to scold
me for my daughter's sleep, the reckless wind.
But two at least came radiant to see us.
I breathe their garden's air, I hear them call
to each other: where red wallflowers burn, to touch
blue larkspur. Help the aged. Help us all.

Draining

Dark summer, they piped the spring.
No one had seen it
but the field tramped to mud,
thistles sprang tall.
Frightening the child
the digger carved the paddock.
Grey pipes with elbows broke through the field wall.
Trickling, tame, the spring has reached the yard.

The water tub spills sour straw.
They are busy in their house.
I fill a huge white bucket from the spring.
Idly the water drizzles down
it is cold as the space at the heart of flame.
I have tasted it, in the thundery air,
will not again.
It is rank as earth

barley field broken by wind
dry cliff where the adder comes
nothing asked for but our strength
tongues of sweat on the smooth back,
ash or white of bone.

On the pipe's lip it is a sheet:
it forks in wind, two glittering tails,
twists in one white thread
the light by which the trees are tossed
hisses in the bucket's cool
and is not lost
and is not lost

Christmas Roses

December. By now, the catalogues will have been sent:
the seeds, the huge Dutch bulbs, and – all that mattered –
   the roses.
Remember them in our offices, spilling off chairs?
on the cover, some lemon-tipped miniature,
or, in a bad year, the latest Mauve Wonder?
Whoever wanted a purple rose? Anyone – sitting in slippers,
or in scuffed boots, gulping dark tea or gold whisky,
who turns, at last, to my catalogue; sees there, my asterisked
   name.

For I am on every list. I bred one rose
with finest tints of apple-flower. I died two years ago.

When I was young there were orchards everywhere: tended.
Then cows were turned in them, square and silk,
snuffling the grey bark, hobbling the dusk.
Then the builders came, who could always plead
the need for more houses. I did not see need
to build in so many orchards.

The rose I grew – page twenty-three –
has crinkled flowers: white veined with red,
in broken lines so fine you'd think
it smudged with pink. Man, use your eyes!

Each year the wind swept off the fen
we set more panes in the great house
which kept my new stock from the frost.
Only Mauve Wonders, then the crafty
packing charges, met our loss.

Now, if my son has let it stand
eyeless to the blackest gales
I do not care – I might be glad.

For in the first year, fresh to death,
I thought: if I had time again
I would have bred a sterner rose,
its white as bare as cloud, or frost,
(but not as smiles that watch the dead).
Or I would grow it scarlet, deep –
never so warm – as hearts' quick blood.

The disillusioned men, who bred
the first tamed roses, willed them hard
as their war colours; crimson throbbed
their chosen petals; purple jarred
against the whiteness of their stock.

As I grew out in my next year
I passed, with winds, across the world.
All I had done, all, once, I loved,
entrusted to the clear walls, whirled
away from me. My roses fed
no living mouth. I stole my bread.

What shall I find in my third year?
The tea-steam blooms along the panes
while tired eyes lose their place, the light's flower closes.
Living, dead, we stay at war. The scratches
black in the glass, were not the work of roses.

March Pigeons

I have wasted ten years. You did not love me, ever.
You laughed at me, but that was long ago.
When I was far, you thought that I might be
A glittering comfort.

They, the two woodpigeons
Sit on one branch, grow dark with afternoon
Or sun licks round a collar. They are preening
Easy as moulting, heavy, grey and slow.
A curl of white, a single feather falls.

As boulders wait, these two are beautiful.
I do not envy stones. The ten years are
Heavy as the feather's drifting star.

Brockhampton

The land was too wet for ploughing; yet it is done.
Even the stones of the ridges lie sulky and brown.
The roads are a slide of mud. The wet sky
Is blank as the chink of the hawk's perfect eye.
A blink before the dark comes down
Drops the peregrine sun.

The land glows like an awkward face.
Broken posts, by which sheep graze
Shine pale as growing wood.
Above, the last crow's wings
Cannot frighten from my blood
The stubborn light of things.

The Queen's Funeral

Her own horse steps in violet silk.
Black velvet sighs upon her bier
The Duchess's train is wide as Thames.
The clerks and diarists crowd near.

Later, too late, they find the note
Forbidding all show. As before,
A practical and honest soul,
She'd spend the money on the poor.

Snow whirls on mud. Each coffee shop,
Warm inn, stands closed. Her heart's one friend –
Bound by custom, strange in grief –
The ruined King does not attend.

Tewkesbury

Tewkesbury fields are flat and dim.
They will build houses there, one school.
We come each Sunday, late, to swim

not in the river's brooding cool
(what is the Abbey looking at?)
but in a clean, blue-cloistered pool.

They fought upon the river flats.
There Henry prayed, devout and mad.
God, what are you looking at?

For Richard comes. There is no mouth
to say if he is animal,
a crooked butcher from the North,

or too is trapped by that raw day
would kiss the jewelled cross; would be King.
One shadow trembles in his way.

Child, is it a proper thing
to wonder if he killed with joy
or as the cat's claw hooks, unthinking?

Would it make you wander, weary
outside the light, the looming tower
in waste of fog at Tewkesbury?

Monks bound the small, holed corpse; remember
his praying did not feed another.
The man who stabbed him might rule better.

But, voices cry, there were the others,
beneath the stone of one more tower,
the smothered children, the two brothers.

They swam no rivers, dived no pools.
The Tower's keeper had my name,
held silent, neither saint nor fool.

The mud-breeched armies were the same,
Henry's or York's, the blindest guess.
But afterwards, outside the game,

the thick hand finds the bony wrist.
The quiet men come for the key.
They walk towards you from the mist,

you see them now, will always see
though swimming in the tranquil pool
of broadest sun, in Tewkesbury.

A Chinese Wedding

A Chinese wedding! On the muddy floor
Of the Peach Orchard Restaurant, the guests, in grey
Winter overcoats stood waiting for
'The bride, Mrs Alison. She is coming,' cried our guide
Who alarmed me, with her hunched good coat,
Her husband, the dark editor. Outside
Snake firecrackers woke the streets with smoke.

The bride towered fire-red: the fabled bird
Which rises from the ash; or as the smoke
Faded, in rich skirts, a scared slim girl.
'She works in the station,' Mrs Zhe declared.
Had I seen her, trousers baggy at the knees
In the dingy panelled waiting rooms
Left, still for Soft Class, by the Japanese?

In her rough book I scrawled 'Congratulations,'
Her father filled my hands with fruited sweets.
Would she grow, like Mrs Zhe, a 'dragon lady,'
Lips closed to question in a fair flushed face?
For terror breaks both sides. 'Now you have seen
Our part,' (she almost sighed) 'you must go south
To the mountains. Rivers there, I think, are clean.'

Red is old danger's colour: blood on books,
The wrong seed, dead in poor ground, Zhou En-lai
'Who did and spoke against his will, because
To save some, to do good, he must endure.'
The girl's small fingers touched, withdrew. Whose son
Lies lost in dark, hands outstretched to that fire?
It licked her sleeves. It once loved everyone.

Overnight

This is the Tangshan sleeper where
the chef sits drunk in the dining car

'There is no gas for heaters' so
the air inside is chill as snow.

In Soft Class, wrapped in grubby piles
of blanket fur, we let the miles

of metal ring our bones and boots,
but cannot sleep, since Chinese flutes

mourn through the speakers everything
the winter child dreamed, sleep till spring.

This dry land, neither small nor kind,
will haunt me when it drops behind

as I sleep, as if dead, until
scuffling wet leaves, the sparrows shrill

who cannot wake the drunken man
upon the sleeper to Tangshan.

Dawn Run

Sunday and so clear a day
That as I drive in rush and strain
I wonder why I cannot rest
To live as easy as the rain.
Fretting under traffic lights
I see a pub sign newly hung,
A glistening picture of a horse
With under it a name. Dawn Run.

She won her race at Cheltenham,
Cleared Gold Cup fences, mile on mile.
The cup her owner waved to us
Blurred mud and strain beneath the smile.
I held her shoe once in my hand,
A broad foot, and a heart to match.
They flew her off to France to win,
But there she fell, and broke her back.

So I remember why it is
I do not pass her brilliant face
To drink and in my ease, forget
The pain that is another place,
That is the cost of any prize.
If we had weighed their price, why then
Who else would taste this perfect day,
How many mares, how many men?

After the X-ray

If he had stayed
in the four white walls
or alone in his patch, the untidy hedge
strewing its roses through empty hours
he would never have met the dark mare
whose neck he licked by the elderflower
whose kick snapped his straight cannonbone.

For sixteen weeks he must stand in the straw
watching the light wash and ebb.
All warmth will have flowed past when he stumbles out
November's wind raw on his leg.
Was it worth it? He shuffles, he cranes to the lane,
calls her, and calls her again.

Hay Fever

For Robyn

Eyes swell, as from a blow; you cry.
I have to fight
To keep your dirty fingers out of eyes
Which almost close
As you stumble past the plumed grass of the lane
The choking elderflower, the painful rose.

What is pollen, anyway? you sniff.
The dusty air
Veined with its passages of gold, as if
You were given presents everywhere.
Summer, for which you longed, to which you raced,
You cannot bear.

The Spring at Chedworth

There is no goddess in the spring
the sturdy walls are bare.
The painted plaster crumbled
colours danced into the air.
The Victorian explorers
found their nymph no longer there.

She would not wait to greet them
though her mouth was never still.
Her baths, where girls sat idly
they miscalled a fulling mill.
'Nymphaeum' fades their labels
where the empty waters spill.

I have seen her in the August yard
shriek, beneath the hose,
leap in a Welsh river
in her rough and sweat-streaked clothes.
But desire runs through her fingers
she is gone as water goes.

She left inside her basin
a black beetle which clasps tight
a bead of air, her glistening gift,
as he spirals out of sight,
as the cuckoo in the wet trees
as her laughter in the night.

On Wistley Hill

Sheep, have you found a shoe?
                              They were not here
when we rode, boisterous, through afternoon.
They lift their bony faces, strangely white
on the long back of the hill. The reservoir
floats bluer than the sky. A Roman snailshell
glints white beside the track. The pale farmhouse,
despite the signs for B &B, shines empty.
Grey ponies in the ridge-fields stand unfed.

I wait for the white moon, swollen and eager,
and, meanwhile, I trudge back, to the beechwood
where we slithered over banks. The Thames starts here,
that proud, foul river, in a slime of root.
Oh, day drops and curved twigs mock in their hardness,
my fingers probe the hoofholes, nothing's there,
not owl or badger or the ghostly sheep.

So much, I think, has drowned beneath the wood,
lovers' hairpins, farmers' iron, pig bones.
Frightened of rape and loss, I almost run
whistling old tunes, beneath the lightless sky.
How short spring's days are, despite all we do.
Where have the sheep gone? Who will find my shoe?

Linum

It is not tall enough, it will not make a crop –
it has changed its name. It used to be flax,
maker of sheets for fine ladies' beds.
Now it is linseed; feeds cattle.
It is high as a knee, blown with threads of leaf,
scattered with flower. What corn is blue?
They are mouths, they are stars, they gleam sweet
as those pictures of children under dark leaf
in frames of deep gilt. It knows nothing;
the sky is bitterer. Last night's sun
was icy lemon, with drifts of grey;
the morning's blaze is for storm. The flax flowers
begin to shimmer, with a metal edge,
to reflect ripe cloud, race a colder sea.
The flies still whirl in hot air, and I
rise quick up the ridge, through the brief, starred fields.
It is not every day you can run through the sky.

After Beethoven

After he died she came, a veiled lady,
Who stood beside the bed. Nothing was said.
(There was a widow, who had had a child.)
She did not brush his forehead with her fingers,
She stood: now robed in fat beneath her furs,
Her veil the dark of time.

When she went home she cried a little, blotched
Her face, then stopped. Her daughter had gone out.
She clasped her hands, with their false ring, and listened.

The bed was warm, but when she reached the street
The keen air made her shawl a cave of white.
Her feet, in their small boots, broke through the snow
Softer, and faster, like a young girl dancing.

He never heard those steps. He quarrelled with her,
Struck her with silence, would not hear her name.
Now she spoke his; and snuffing out the candle,
Listened to the echo he became.

Out of Hanoi

I had been happy in this country.
The sun had glinted, waitresses were young,
Black ponytails brushed for their next promotion,
They brought us the land's fruit, gold jars of jam.
The lizard flicked, past the courtyard pool.
Country of water! Then out of the mist's ocean

A huge rat bobbed along the parapet,
It vanished into nothing. Dozing in the coach
For the first time I heard the mud
Past the tarmac and the roadside stalls
Suck down below lush bristled ranks of rice.
For the first time, I feel the dead:

The French below the paddies, the burnt pilots,
The children's nestled bones. They died for nothing.
The planes flew home. New shops spring up, each pane
Of plastic heavy with America.
I leave the misted coach, with a dry throat.
The living sell me water, in warm rain.

All

And all who died, from winter's sleet,
From flu, from guns, from cells grown wrong,
Still stand, one breath from fingers' reach,
Just out of touch, all colour gone.

The dead grow smaller. From a train
Mist takes the fields, drinks green to grey,
The fog has swept across their face.
In yard or park, they walk away,

Then wait in rooms, without a fire,
With tea uncleared, without a fuss;
In cushioned chairs, now closer drawn,
Nod to each other, not to us.

But in mid age it is not strange
To glimpse them, in the windy street,
Quiet at the kerb, who are all dead,
From guns, cruel cells, or winter's heat.

The Bride Who Fell Asleep

She slept before her wedding.
She dozed inside the car
Cold leather to her hot cheek
She did not travel far.
Strange ghost of influenza
The sleeping sickness came.
It took away her voice and laugh
It only left her name.

I do not even have her name.
I smell the leather. Think
You know the currents in that pool
Where she brought to the brink
White flowers, foolish slippers.
She never reached the hall
Caught his quick laugh, and then her voice,
The red-haired girl next door.

I yawn; I lean against the door
Through which she could not go.
I shout at sullen children
I grimace at the snow.
She missed the war's fresh fires,
The shops' crammed shelves which break
Our children's hearts in silence.
I whisper to her, 'Wake'.

Woods

They are too frail. They will not grow in England.
In the bare islands where the trees lie felled,
Brown bays of wood, the autumn crocuses
Shoot tough white stalks to startling purple throats.

There have been on this farm in recent years
Three suicides, two broken marriages.
More trees stand marked for felling. Dumb
Before the gale, the splintering of branches
With arch of throat, the autumn crocus come.

Display

You were the fireworks' soft blooming
Which etched the eye, which made the throat gasp 'Ah!'
Nothing was left but fine gold dust, which sifted
A starless black. The crowds disperse,
My sleeve breathes smoke; all is the same;
My hair turns grey; my daughter soars;
My heart still stops to hear your name.

Now

Now she has gone
closed in a jar
as paper rustles round seeds.
For fifty years she has lived alone
with her husband and child
by the London streets.
Now she is free to fly home.

Like a lift of the heart
the plane shadows the Alps,
as a hand crosses wrinkled skin,
back to the broad streets, enamel stoves
the white slope crowded with pine.
Scatter me back to the sun and the wind.
In the snow of the bed, he wakes,
no bird, no pulse
but her blind return.
We were never earth.
Our dust aches.

Postcard

Another meeting that we never had
was in the South resort where we
both went, separately, to work,
where wedding-cake hotels and sea
are not the hot glint of its name:
Brighton, with Sandra's crumpled card
in the first newsagent's you meet,
where tongues touch ice cream, in a Sunday fog
still roughened by the cooling sheets.
There never was a better place
not to see you, as your face
quieter, younger, stared across
the pebbles' sleek collapsing cliff
past shaking dogs, red blowing coats,
where the waves' long shine and lift
praise to me, in their shameless stir
all that you are, and never were.

Webs

And then the spiders' silk. It covered lawns
In leaping lines. Across October's heat
It ran like water through the windy light.
I did not touch or test it with my feet.
It danced, as insects swarmed. It twitched. It beat.

Beside the wood, you said, new ploughland lay
With clay and stones cast up in heavy files.
In the last surge of sun you saw the same
The bare earth shiver with the spiders' trials.
One acre shimmered open, miles on miles.

Staying at Furnace Farm

All houses have noises. In Maggie's old house
I hear a rush. It is taps, I think, water.
Unsteady with dreams, I go to the window.
No rain beats the curtains. The night is half over.

I have heard time.
She ran down the stairs
like a girl to her lover.

On the Road

The rag is the squirrel. Grey screamer at magpies,
tree-flyer, tail-snapper, he's gone.
His airy bounds met the final car.
He could have stepped safely, lived long.
but he left the soft air for the dangerous earth.
I do not say he was wrong.

End of the Day

As I fill the trough, the waters tremble.
The wasps come down,
Jasmine-yellow, ticked with black, and loud.
One drinks, spread-eagle. Tail twitches
With what might –
If a human finger beat – be thought delight.
One drops a straw leg; drifts.
Buzzed shimmer there
Of frantic wings restore it to dry air,
As helicopters lift, above a war.
At lapping edge
Three wasps whine into quarrel on a ledge.

Hill sky is combed by heat. The air is dull
With harvest clouds. Yet look. The trough brims full.

In the General

The anaesthetist seems to bounce off the walls.
It is very late. As if underground
The trolley with my daughter crawls
With her ruined appendix. Wide and blue
The gowned anaesthetist's speech is strange.
As he pats each wall, words flash from true.

His accent is thick as the paint's veined white
On the glimmering walls. He comes, I think,
From a country where thought ducked, down from sight.
'Have we a surgeon?' he asks the nurse
Who starts, then laughs. My daughter's lids flash.
In the building's bowels, her quiet grows worse.

'I have no knowledge of surgeons,' insists
His voice. She sighs, tugs doors apart,
A number swings from my daughter's wrist.
Rooms shine with tubes. In self-defence
I glance away, then I translate.
He means, he has no confidence.

He knows, I know, there should be cries
So terrible the air would stop.
They struggle with the drip, which dries.
'She's out.' As voices drown in water,
Night hides the unimagined day
I shout in anger at my daughter.

Turing's Bicycle

Dear Alan Turing, my knowledge is slight.
I read somewhere: when your bicycle chain
Shook loose, you would not fix it tight

You pedalled, you counted. At forty-one
Before the chain links rattled free
You sprang to the dust. You hooked them on.

You cracked war's codes, the mind's machine.
But you died young, by your own hand.
The chain unspooled in its oily sheen.

Such scanty signs. What to infer?
That we, less thoughtful than you were
Must hammer chains; re-code despair.

Elizabeth of York

Courted by Richard III; married to Henry VII

Item: more silver to pawn.
Item: the blue gown to mend.
Item; a fair child born.

Item: a husband, no friend,
Courteous, constant, and mean.
Item: his mother, who sends

Grown children away. In the hour
Their black envoys call, I taste pity;
She is safe; who desires no power.

The river lies frozen. I see
The wasted list strike to a flare,
To sputtered ash. He wanted me.

That winter spun misrule's season,
The hall-fires flung red, as my hair,
More generous. I had left prison

Of the sanctuary church. I was free.
In a world of terrible colour
His gaze enfolded me

Then his hands on my breasts. In their quiet
My brothers lay under the stair.
He drew me from the dance's riot,

He gave me a dress of that colour
He had given his sick wife: flame,
Silk, hair, great fires' glimmer.

I burnt it: with the crackle
Old collars use when starched,
At my mother's word, in our lodging
As Henry's army marched.

I knew his prayer: damnation,
Or snatched, to dazzling day.
To kill: be torn by thorn trees.
Is there no other way?

The careful gown is mended.
I pray, from brutal sin.
I pull the patched wool over,
The silk peels off my skin.

Canals

They carried coal. The black-maned horses sweated.
They carried corn, which hissed into the mills.
They carried slates, to patch out winter rain,
Then hot manure, for which men paid no tolls.

And, smoother than a swan, they carried china,
Pale blue and black, Josiah Wedgwood's best.
White lovely youths, with naked goddesses,
Glided unfingered in their tissued nest.

The water leaked in silence through the banks.
The bargeman coughed, in the unceasing rain.
Warm horse, bright coal, bankrupt canal are gone.
Flesh melts to snow. The gods' slow smiles remain.

Wright

Wrapped in a blanket, he slept by his plane.
He ate from a can. Was the new paintwork dry?
Life could not be quite as simple again.

The damp French breeze blustered. He would not fly,
Though the crowds swarmed around him, rebellious as bees,
He tugged at his cap. He did not mean to die.

Wind hammered his eyes. He peered down, through thin trees,
Found his angle for landing. Soon it would be done.
His patents would free him from dangers like these.

Did the high air excite him? The glance of the sun?
The patents destroyed him. Unmarried, much sued,
He died of exhaustion before they were done.

The machine runs on patience. If you would ride
Each nut must be tightened, each weld checked again,
By the silent and steady man, bent to its side.

At the Beginning

It was the time of bombs, or rumours of them,
When ash from burnt towers fell upon the lips
Like an unanswered prayer. From your great height
You know what we did then

Whether we fought long wars, so young men died
In the cold passes; if the solid shops,
Bus stations, rose in dust; if our great planes
Blazed on the mountainside.

Trust me, it was a time when we would start
At dusked skin of a wrist, at a plane's drone.
I could predict, unsleeping, their success.
The war was theirs. The terror was our own.

Epigrams

My Latin has left me,
which may be as well.
They were brute engineers
and their afterlife, hell.

Only one tag stays:
a bird with no wings.
'In medias res'
in the middle of things.

I am weighed down by parents,
made mad by my child.
The late sky is sleeting
the garden is wild.

I slump on a chair
in the last glow day brings.
In medias res
in the muddle of things.

Self-set

It is the wild cranesbill
Seed stolen from the hedge.
It opens mouths of warm blue
White whispers at its edge.

As in this strange wet summer
The sodden, tame rose lists
It glimmers light. As rain itself
It stubbornly persists.

It is the wild cranesbill.
The lost are gone with you.
It neither owns nor saves us.
Its cups glow clearest blue.

The Blue Door

The door swings slowly to one side.
As people cough before the play
A rectangle of blue light rides

Behind the stage. There's nothing there
But dust and cold, the little comb
Which slipped from the last dancer's hair

Which she will never see again:
The glow on dunes the child saw,
Sea's plain beyond, then the sky's pane

Above the lover's bed, the cry
Of day reflected back again:
A blue square in the baby's eye.

The light grows richer, stills then thins.
The dark is quiet. The play begins.

On the Second of August

Oh I am very tired, but the old horse is dead
I had for eighteen years.
He was twenty-eight. Do you like horses?
One day you will be dead.

His coat shone red; the tumour in his eye
also flared red.
He lowered his head kindly.

You will not be shot, as the old horse was shot,
at nine o'clock in the wheat field
as the light wind drew from the south
as the light rain rustled hay
and he died with corn in his mouth.

Calf Sound

You heard the seal upon its rock
Neither fish nor deer
Black and glossy, silk of sea
Its cry rose clear

A lilting voice, a keening
The wind ran in that call
The white song that a bone blew
The love in it would kill.

You will not be a kind mother
Or faithful to your kin
If you stay on the cropped green turf.
Come in. Come in.

The hut has clouded windows
Kettles, dry plates, strong tea.
Your black eyes swim with moon's light
The dripping track to sea.

Mithras and the Milkman

Mithras Lord of the Sun has killed the bull,
The soldiers praise him.
In the North-East he stopped the wall of wind.
Upon Thames' banks he carved the muddy cave.
The soldiers praised him

Who stole him from the Persians. On the way
His red-hot birth was dulled to Christmas Day.

On Boxing Day the milkman sails through dark.
Whine of the motor cuts inside his head.
He lost his wife, a son and several teeth,
My note 'Two, please'. Three pints crash down instead.
I wake in sweat, wrestle through tangled sheets.
He climbs the cab's hot cave. The bull is dead.

Flight

It was bright and fat
As it fluttered the grass.
Cat rattled the fence, rushed
Its spilt sun, the brass

Of its light voice; as I ran
My cloth flapped. It flew.
Hail raked through the gardens.
The sky burned steel-blue.

All day I think of it
While at Europe's edge
The refugees pause.
Child sleeps by a hedge.

So in a third country
Whose words will not rhyme
By a warm foreign body
Far out of my time

Someone thinks of a room
The cage they left; still
The canary bursts dark
With its bubble and trill.

At Home

Mr Handel's friend comes to dinner.
They dine upon ordinary fare.
Handel slips into a sideroom.
His friend creeps up on him there.

He guzzles the finest claret.
He rips a chicken's white breast.
In a bare room lit by mirrors
Handel forgets his guest.

Scratching down music will blind him.
Enormous, lonely and odd,
In the clouded gilt of his mirror
George Handel nods to God.

Homework. Write a Sonnet. About Love?

There are too many sonnets about love.
First let us name, then freeze, their eager faults.
(Who is it whistles, piercingly, above?
By the dark fields, the engine shudders, halts.)
No lover ever worried about fame,
More than the pearls, which tumbled round her ears.
(It might be Russia, when the quick thaw came;
Down steel steps, with a bundle, she appears.)
Nor were they ever read without a yawn;
The one who longed for them received no word.
(Behind her fall the lights of the low town.
She leaves the tracks. She whistles like a bird.)
The sonnet has no room to make an end,
The poplars dance. She takes the sudden bend.

Tess

I hate the book, except the end
In which the lovers break
Into an empty house and lie
In dust and warmth and ache

Inside the endless minutes.
The clothes sleep on the floor.
The soft old woman sent to clean
In silence shuts the door.

She is half-deaf and yet she hears
Men tramp with steady feet.
The rider thuds the clearing's shade.
The black cars block the street.

Holiday

Christmas. I go back to bed with a fig
Whose belly is plump and swollen with seeds,
Crisp, gold as small fires, yet in each one
Is something dark and thick, which needs
To linger and be kept with care.
For the days are short, then the mornings start
Darker, as we freeze and work.
Earth fills the seeds at the lost fig's heart.

Tabby

You played upon the driveway,
You tapped the leaves' dry skin
Your brother blocked the cat flap
To stop you bounding in.

I finished with the paper,
Its cartoons and its cares.
I walked in the bright hallway.
You sat upon the stairs.

How had you crossed the kitchen?
When had the flap slammed flat?
You stared at me unblinking.
Death is a quiet cat.

The Card

Divorce comes close to death. I knew them at sixteen.
They sent each other Mars Bars through the post
Which the sorting rollers crushed. I think the priest
Who married them is dead; but he died young.
How she laughed before her wedding, deep-throated in
    the porch.

Houses grew bigger, and their elder son
Mounted disaster; but for thirty years
Their garden filled with butterflies, and cake
On rocking tables. Last time, her black bitch
Nervous from rescue, tailed her everywhere.
Its sheepdog's eyes shone rimmed with brilliant white.

I ought to cut our grass, but cannot think.
I sink upon the stairs as in a fog,
I hunt for the address. 'Is autumn free?
I'll see you then. I'm fine. I kept the dog.'

Cycles

Would I go back? The childhood bike
Was secondhand, painted thick blue.
Yet scratch the hedge, dull black showed through.
I rattled blank lanes where I liked.
I had a college bike, caught hard
In its top gear, when I met you.
Uphill, I fought for every yard.

When I first worked, roads gave more space.
I steered cheap bikes through tall streets, full
Of selfish hopes, the first air cool.
Some came, some went. Sun scorched my face.
I whirred electric windows down.
Caught in the traffic's throb and pull
I drove my daughter into town.

This bike is new. It shines and purrs.
I shake, but can still pedal, swoop
From our workshop's door in crazy loops
Behind old roofs. My fine gears whirr,
I set off home. Lit trees storm past,
Late rain holds off, stiff knees hold out.
Oh never have I gone so fast.

Severe Weather Warning

The walls are firm. The central heating hums,
Cars wait; but I am a slave to weather.
I sit in clouded light. The forecast comes,
The horse is miles away, on the harsh hills.
Storms will strike us; as the sodden leather
Slips from my fingers, as the branch-fall kills

The young girl in her soft-topped car. At home
My dearest projects wait for kinder air.
New bulbs, adrift on Latin names like foam,
Float in their box. They should be anchored in
The tideless ground: dark arums, sleek as hair
Under hoods. Earth lies too wet for trampling.

Others are free, detached. They watch their screens,
They drive to drinks with friends. I watch the sky,
Its maddening dazzle and its lemon streams
Of sun through rain's dark tails. By the poor school
Soaked starlings wheel from oaks. They scatter high.
I live in the wind's thrust, by the sun's rule.

But why? I left the country. Join the town.
The soil beneath the drive tugs at my heel.
This is like trusting luck, whirled high, cast down.
It is. But weather has a fierce ghost.
Its wet black wing has touched my face. I feel
It breathe, stretch, wake, before quick cars and toast.

The Lincolnshire Accent

It is a voice even in men
Turned hesitant
A child who now has lost the note
His mother sent.
It starts in warmth but then the vowels
Begin to blur,
Give words no end. A lamb's wide cries
Crumble to air.
My uncle's voice, my grandfather's
Sift quiet through death
A Scunthorpe girl speaks on the news.
I hold my breath.

The North Room

I have seen unhappiness, who stood
In a high Oxford room, beside my bed.
The room was narrow. I think she was a maid.
She certainly was dead.

It was that time of darkness, when you wake
Tunnelled from morning, half-choked by despair.
There was no lace, or whispered words to take:
A thickening of the air

Which brushed against the lips, caught in the throat,
Cleared, with the buzzing of a midnight fly.
Next term I had the front room. It shone west.
I swung the bed to sky.

Edward Thomas's Daughter

Now winter prowls upon the hills
I write to her, her head so old
The war before the last war fills
Her mind. She lists her father's songs.

A man, I tell her, I admire:
Who steps as close as a lost child.
They sang, she tells me, by the fire
Wild Army songs before he died.

My fingertips once touched that world.
I saw it linger, washing boil,
The fire chill as long ashes curled.
Will Russia's gas put out our lights?

The robin brushes me at dusk.
Our good bones fail. We leave no mark.
His voice, she writes, was clear and quiet.
I hear him singing in the dark.

Prepositions

Through, in, over, out.
Who else troubles about

Such little words? Sail past,
You solid nouns, the blast

Of verbs drives you to sea.
Adjectives glide, still lovely.

But icebergs glare and face.
Why hack at frozen space

Unless I come to you,
Over, out and through?

Puff

You leapt up, the computer's cat, then curled
On your own chair, before a glowing world
Of spidered text and viruses, would wait
Calmly, in paper drifts, as I worked late.
You tongued your ruff smooth, kept your grave eyes round,
Sniffed coffee, chocolate, till an end was found,
Or slept, sleek squirrel, in your feathered tail
So when I scooped you up, your long paws trailed,
Your chin lolled on my wrist, flowed warm past fear.
I do not think, in all your fourteen years,
You knew unkindness. But the tumour grew,
You blinked black lids to lamps as we walked through.
What sun or screen is now too bright for you?

Commuter

The siren wails across the bridge,
September's shadow sails the ridge,

The small blue car and you have gone
To Gloucester in the awkward sun

To your first job, demanding screens,
Choked copiers, your colleagues' screams.

The siren dips then fades away
Past mist-fumed fields, the motorway.

Once, under a striped jeep's canvas
You saw an elephant lunge at us.

As the lone motorcycle roared
The pony reared, then threw you hard.

There have been planes and swimming pools,
Bicycles swerving right from schools.

On wind, the last long note is spun,
Heart clenched for the most dangerous run
To Gloucester, in the steady sun.

High Notes

Over the ridge, flooded tracks snarl with ice.
February shifts through its angles of wind,
North to the bare ash, east to the numbed hand.
Above the torn pasture, the buzzard's voice.

The buzzard is many birds. Dropped to the road
It rips the soft rabbit with eagle's hard glare.
As kite, it circles through ceilings of air.
It sleeps in the ash like a ruffled brown toad.

Its voices are many, a mewing prattle,
A languorous whistle over the wood.
Once, when the lambs tottered banks, it could
Draw from its throat a machine gun's rattle.

Now its voice has changed, though the night is bringing
The sun's red disc, the moon's white eye.
Its call swoops and breaks. Its mate hovers by.
To frozen acres the buzzard is singing.

Three

There must have been a doorstep once
Where those three met and spoke,
His mad red curls, her jaunty scarf,
His thin wrists, long black coat.
I never knew them, never was
As young as they were when
Drunk with hope – and a little more –
They knew each other then.

One broke into a bawdy song.
She shook her head, beguiled,
Then pushed him down the rain-black steps.
Even the sad one smiled.
Rain on the shoulder, rain on lips,
Her coat warm as a hen
She lent one money, one a kiss,
They knew each other then.

What is known, in today's hard sun,
Is all too quickly said.
He drank. She lost her lovely voice.
The quiet one is dead.
The dog rose, heart-shaped in its thorns,
Shivers upon the stem
Glints perfect, shatters at my touch,
Never and always, then.

Schemes

Who plants forsythia now? It is not tasteful;
Too ragged, tall, and dull when leaves are out.
But see the sparrows rush into its heart,
Eyes stroke it, raw and golden as a shout.

The Jane Austen Reader

Welcome to the truth. Miss Bingley married Darcy.
Louisa skipped down steps, intact in pink.
Elizabeth grew fat. Anne Elliott took to drink.

But no, you cry. No truth. These deal with love.
They are the books we love. They must be right
To block, like hoods, the crowded glare of trains
Or read alone in bed on Christmas night.

Provision

The horses of the First World War
Shipped out to Egypt with the drafts,
Sold, without oats or tack, were found
Starved, scabbed, in Cairo, between shafts.

A charity gave less cruel bits,
Vets, water troughs, to slake some pain.
The ribbed sides had sunk, finally,
When the troopships sailed East again

With cavalry horses, all hand-picked,
Big in bone, packed hard with oats.
A groom I knew marched through Iraq
To haul their buckets, shine their coats.

That war too ended. There they stood,
Sixteen hands high, without a spot
On their smooth shoulders – Do not say
Soldiers learn nothing. They were shot.

6.25

My day begins with darkness
Since I get up too soon.
Hung vast above the garage end
A brilliant moon

Ignores the morning radio,
White sea without an ebb
Freezes the lithe ash twigs
A glittered web.

The light is metal, deep and pure.
It is what Plato's cave
Ached for, truth, the throb of power
His shadows gave.

It borrows from the animals
Snow of the owl's wing
Flash of the badger's white cheek, wet
From tunnelling.

Gleams slide from gutter, shed and slate,
The radio plays on.
I burn my toast. The East turns blue.
The moon has gone.

The Inn for All Seasons

I will stop here for coffee:
And in its dark perfume
Halfway upon my journey
They step into the room

The one who could not love me
Smiles, slips twenty years.
My old horse whinnies, rideable,
His quick mind washed of fears.

My tabby cat, no longer thin
Races the summer wind.
And I recall each urgent thing
My long sleep left behind,

My child without her sorrows
Long grass without chill dew,
My mother's name, that shopping list,
What I must say to you.

Here is the gate, here is the chance
The calm dark rooms will give.
The bend flies up before me.
I steer away, and live.

The Beanfields' Scent

It is light as winds, without coldness,
Fresh waves of sea without salt,
It blows a sweet honey, uncloying,
It is happiness without fault.

Its flowers' tongues ask no taxes,
Though their purple is royal; their white
Is pressed by black so pure
That noon is burned by night.

Who buys a scent called 'Beanflowers'?
Its glossy blue of leaf
Buckles, to June's sharp showers.
Best things are free and brief.

Levellers' Day

The Levellers came to Burford
They wanted land and votes.
They clattered down the small streets
With fresh mud on their coats.

Only one war was over.
They swept past Cromwell's men.
'We should have fought them by the stream.'
Luck does not come again.

They fell into the inn's soft beds
As dead men sink through earth.
Then Cromwell came, who did not sleep,
Who marched them to the church.

They huddled. From the pulpit
Their General told them why
They would be shipped to Ireland
And which of them must die.

Four men stood in the churchyard,
In first sharp scent of may
One screamed out like a child,
Then tried to run away.

One called the name of Liberty
Who waits, who never runs.
One lifted up his face and turned
In silence to the guns.

The last, who had grown cunning
Recanted and was spared
To babble from the pulpit
Of how the rest had erred.

Three men sprawled in a churchyard.
Now, in their name, we would
Sing sad songs, then chew soya.
The Levellers tasted blood.

But there is honour in this,
The slow song in the throat.
Three men lie in the churchyard
But we drive home to vote.

Solo

How can the oboe
Sing like a woman?
The long hair flows
Down the player's back.

How can he – yes, he –
Hold breath so long?
Young planets flee
The black horizon.

Dew gleams the long slopes
Of the park.
The notes fly fast
As bees from dark.

Wrap me in sleep
Toss down this care
A tumbled tune
A glistening hair.

Scraper: John Clare's name for a fiddler

Clare noted down the gypsy's tune,
Not fire's white ash, the beer-blurred moon,
Loud nights spent with the gypsies.

His life dragged to its untuned end,
The London trips, new soft-voiced friends,
Women more used than gypsies.

He scarcely worked. More children came.
Carriages left. He lost his name.
How neat his music's pages,

Gavottes and sea songs, waltzes, jigs,
No clag of ploughland, reek of pigs.
Their notes flew off his pages.

How fast Clare bowed. He touched each string
Tenderly as a bird's spread wing.
His sons forsook the fiddle,

Ran the railways, left for good.
Did his wife stroke her apron smooth,
Without regret or anger

Reach down the fiddle by its dumb throat
Take, gratefully, the folded note?
He lived too long a stranger.

But the fine casing cracked with use,
Bundled across the inns, strings loose.
From his low chair, half-tipsy

He slung his silver, spent no word,
Tucked under arm, a sleeping bird,
The fiddle swung. Hedge shadows stirred
A sudden tune, unbroken, heard.
He whistled, loped, the gypsy.

Visitors

Hummingbird hawkmoths hover.
Tawny wings – grey bodies – blur.
Three-inch tongues whip and flutter
Valerian's rose-pink flower,
Mauve spires of buddleia.
The bees ignore them, dapper
Workers fed winter sugar,
Humped bumblebees, who stagger
To line cold clay with nectar.
Both hawkmoths speed to cover.
Cautiously, like a swimmer,
A bee begins to hover.

December 25th, 12 noon

No, honestly, we are more organised than we look.
The piles of clothes are all washed.
I have fed the birds, then the cats,
Now the cats are out: catching birds,
It starts to unravel. The cream will not whip,
It mocks the whisk in white hissing waves.
The cat flies the long grass, scattering wings,
The creased pale blouses shiver and fall.
Time, I think, to drink, then wander
The flooded footpaths, to waver and call
And Christmas, and Merry, and to you all.

Xerxes, an Opera

It is utterly lovely and I am asleep.
For years I have watched them, nodding away
Through poems, percussion, the old, as the young snigger
With dark pony-tailed boys, like my daughter's lost love.
They are here today; am I the only
Middle-aged soul? And I am asleep.

I surface through the slime. You are away.
You hate opera. My daughter is unhappy.
It is the hottest June an over-heated world can give.
The chair is hard. I could be in our shabby kitchen
By the radio, with the cat's snores. But I am here,
Risen to lukewarm air. What have I said?

Nothing. Sleep is silent. The flute is silk,
The voices wander air
We cannot breathe; they are their element, birds
Who need no branches. I have no story,
No synopsis. I will see it later,
All plots, sub-plots, Romilda, Arsamenes,
Flower-sellers; an ache in Handel's head.
At the interval, I will slop weak coffee, smile
At the tight-toed ladies, in my easy shoes.
But now I have swum through; sad youth, long age,
Where sleep tugs down, down.
Here is the voice, that easy bird,
The air is cool, I am awake.
It is utterly lovely.

Lapwings

They were everywhere. No. Just God or smoke
is that. They were the backdrop to the road,

my parents' home, the heavy winter fields
from which they flashed and kindled and uprode

the air in dozens. I ignored them all.
'What are they?' 'Oh – peewits – ' Then a hare flowed,

bounded the furrows. Marriage. Child. I roamed
round other farms. I only knew them gone

when, out of a sad winter, one returned.
I heard the high mocked cry 'Pee – wit,' so long

cut dead. I watched it buckle from vast air
to lure hawks from its chicks. That time had gone.

Gravely, the parents bobbed their strip of stubble.
How had I let this green and purple pass?

Fringed, plumed heads (full name, the crested plover)
fluttered. So crowned cranes stalk Kenyan grass.

Then their one child, their anxious care, came running,
squeaked along each furrow, dauntless, daft.

Did I once know the story of their lives?
Do they migrate from Spain? Or coasts' cold run?

And I forgot their massive arcs of wing.
When their raw cries swept over, my head spun

With all the brilliance of their black and white
As though you cracked the dark and found the sun.

Bath Cubes

Lily of the valley, Devon violet, English rose
brought crumpled foil, white silk's swirl, the gurgled
    names of those
great-aunts and godmothers, Edie, Phil and Gwen,
like the coarse white bath cubes, which will not come
    again

with harsh and gritty powder, oiled steam, the after-reek,
jasmine sliding past the river fish (then few) who did not
    speak.
I measured them like love, a flowering of the self,
not the final desperate present plucked quickly from the
    shelf

which no one told me then. No one ever told my toes,
creased and flushed from chilling water as the bathroom
    window froze,
lost in mists of fake French lavender, false lilac, summer
    rose.

The Trent Rises, 1947

When you heard the water whisper
in Crown Yard and Sailors' Alley,
when your husband saw the river
no longer lazy – swollen, free;
what did you grab, to take with you upstairs?
What would I take with me?

Would I snatch letters from the flood,
so their clearest lines and kisses
did not meet condoms, tampons, mud?
Save bills? Saucepans? Water misses
no hidden, plastered wire. No kettle could
boil. The fusebox hisses.

Computers, in a leaky boat?
They hauled fresh water, tins. The swell
of river made the hall a moat.
Tortoise to bucket! Chickens fell
into their bath. Aboard the Co-op's milk float,
the pigs raised merry hell.

The Lunch Box

Though my mother is dying, you buy vegetarian cheese.
There is celery – did you grow it? The rolls are sliced twice,
wrapped in plastic, then foil. They must have taken hours.
I nibble them on the coach. I keep the paper napkin
with all its frantic flowers.

Fruit in February

My mother dead. What did she leave?
Dry days of frost, a weight to grieve.
The dead wake us with worries,
sour milk, the universe.

The hedge beneath the house was thick
with fruit, which gave the glow of milk,
the child's dream. She snatched fingers,
mother's nightmare: 'Pois-on-ous.'

Birth, death, we sleep from dream to dream.
Beside my path to work, a gleam;
the same bush; the shadowed house,
though birds shout, traffic murmurs.

No, these small globes are not pure light
but crazed with brown. Flaws hurt her sight.
The dead leave us their worries,
white fruit for birds, snowberries.

The Shed

He looked after tools, not just his own,
palm-polished handles, Victorian elm,
stamped with initials for John Maidens Barnes

my grandmother's father, who never bought farms,
but his own clutch of ditch-tools. Reach down the hoe

a blacksmith beat for the left-handed twist
of his father, the shepherd, who weeded bean rows
in after-work dazzle, the pipe's long blue mist.

How far they have travelled. This death is still raw.
Shallots' small worlds, held by knots of string,

spin as I brush them. I unhook the fork
he had wiped clean. Soil's finest grains cling.
Though I know it is sun, swept through glass, over land,

the handle grips hot as his palm to my hand.

At Eighty

Spanker, Sharper, Prince and Bob
were horses that my father drove
through rain, through clay, down car-free roads
the workless tramped, for his first job.

He told me as we waited, bored,
outside my dozing mother's ward
Bob kicked him sailing down the yard.

Bob also bolted from the tree,
dragged with clanked chain. The closest shave
came when he swayed back, peacefully,

legs tapping Spanker's sun-warm side,
back to the hay, from dinner break.
The great grey Belgian reared beside,

horse, cart, crashed toppling like a tree.
The shaft's kink saved his battered sides.
Six Irish shearers dragged him free.

A bungalow's quiet bedroom took
breath neither weight nor war could rob.
Out of the dark with patient feet
came Spanker, Sharper, Prince and Bob.

Your Signature Is Required

Oh reading wills I mourn them:
my father's upright hand,
careful from the village school.
So his father wrote; his mother
shaped child's letters, crimped like pastry,
pinched, like the cowslip's petal.
Who will write like that again?
And then, her zeros,
more trouble than a pleasure,
lawyer's chill trick, a second will,
the day my mother slept.

But the tax is saved. I sign
in my slanted dashing hand.
I walk the broad path, common,
to the hill we do not own.
The bramble's flowers raise storms,
palest golds, rough creams and browns,
the gatekeepers, the butterflies
of hottest harsh July.

So I know that they are safe,
so, forgetting them, I pass
a C of moon so tender
she must not be glimpsed through glass.

On the Aerial

Starling is numerous, holds in his throat
the many colours of his oily coat.
Each year he – like his fathers – finds new noise,
wolf-whistles tall as boys,
the phone's trill, then the shriek
of Kirsty, loudest child in all our street.
Tonight he softly mews. Then through his voice are poured
jay, blackbird's honey, thrush-lilts. He, half-heard,
tilts at faint stars, is Spring, is every bird.

Leap Year

In February, in the dark time
from pancakes' smoke to Easter's shine

in Friday's rush, at ten to four,
a driver tapped our workshop door,

turned to the truck. I heard high wind
whistle the cliffs of flats behind.

I went to prop our own door wide.
He was a small man, heavy-eyed,

who spoke of rain, leaned in his truck.
I saw the great steel door blow back,

sweep at him like a guillotine.
I shouted. He leapt back in time.

'It would have crushed his spine, his head.
He would have died', my husband said.

Instead, he carried trays of screws,
drove off inside the roar of news.

The twenty-ninth, the lightless west,
rained on my face. I stood, was blessed.

Victoria Coach Station, 11 p.m.

Two girls stumble, drunken friends.
'Going now? Where's our vodka?'

They drag out matching scarves,
baguettes, crumbs' silk.
                            As if on ice,

claws skid, beaks bob. How I love pigeons,
filthy, joy-filled, precise.

May Day, 1972

How gold it was, the first wash of sky
as voices floated from the tower
as you spun the umbrella the tourists loved,
on every spike a paper flower.

How cold it was at the day's mid-point
when tiredness kicked in like a mule
when you stood at work and the hours stretched
as sea in fog's breath, tense and dull.

How rich and dark was the crumb of cake
which came from the tin of the dancing men
in absurd white clothes: for luck, new life.
How nothing was the same again.

John Wesley's Horse

Riding from barn door to beach,
John Wesley practised what he preached.

Though horses were tight-reined in town
he let his own stretch its neck down,
to snatch, on clifftops, clover, thyme,
frail rose and tooth-brown dandelion.

John Wesley, I face deeper night.
I stare into the same blind light.
I wish you, in the empty hearse,
Your horse's heaven. You could do worse.

In the Black Country

for Roy Palmer

Brush the sooted trees at Cradley,
tramp the ironworks' ash at Brierley,
taste the coal-dust, swirled
round pitheads for the Earl of Dudley
whose miners stole for weekend loot
bronze pheasants from the airy woods
my grandfather helped pen for shoots,
another world.

Visitors plucked one branch of hell.
Gas seeped, ropes snapped, the bad seam fell
on John Dawes, twenty-three.
Women in sackcloth swore as well
as miners. Clean, in the chain shop,
they watched the anvil, levered up
bar for the hammer's perfect drop,
iron like toffee.

Songs, then strikes, then deportations:
praise all who risked for fair conditions,
all who took part.
Smog lifts from China's power stations.
Who was the girl who sat alone
high on the coach, watched chimneys loom,
who cried for joy, since this was home?
Oh my black heart.

Thermal

Sulis Minerva, they found your stone head
in Bath, where my daughter drove me today,
half-Roman, half-Celt. Do not lecture. Instead
we wade through blue pools from the sulphurous spring
in a bubble of freedom, my fifty-fourth birthday,
in rooftop baths, by the gulls' wavering.

How hard she works, my dark Grecian daughter,
hands clenched on the wheel, quick glint of her rings,
marriage, new job. How heavily water,
oiled by the sulphur, smoothes each winter limb.
Roman pipes pump to a Celtic languor.
By rose-red chimneys, I rise and swim.

Sulis Minerva, they took both your names
into the dark which I fear will come back.
When you rose into daylight, girls' eyes shone the same
with shivering shoulders which longed for the south.
With rough hair of weed, eyes sunken and black,
water, not word, wash us warm through your mouth.

At Needlehole

How lovely the land lies in October,
still as the moon.
The new wheat is planted.
The drivers are gone
to pile up their wood
or be soothed by a screen.

The felled tree is sawn,
the robin's cross cry
now liquid and long,
uncannily high.
The cold finds my fingers.
The moon finds the sky.

The Beatles in Hamburg

I was a child, they were grown;
now I am grown, and three are dead.
The German girl who watched them said
'Boys in leather! Beautiful boys!'

She loved the one who turned his back
upon the crowd, painted all night,
murmured 'So sorry' – then collapsed.
The flier pays the fare for flight.

I love the ones they never were.
There was a man in Liverpool
who told them, like rough boys at school,
to wear French suits and trim their hair.

They could not stay in those wet streets
where prostitutes would lean and yawn,
the filthy room with flags for quilts,
the raucous laugh, the German dawn.

I cannot stay too late. One song
ripped and roared into their ears,
caught – Lennon mourned – the Hamburg years
when war seemed over, night stretched long,
but peace lay short-lived. Play that song.

NOTE: The group then included Stuart Sutcliffe, who died in Germany.
The track singled out by John Lennon is 'I Saw Her Standing There'.

Wilfred Owen at the Advanced Horse Transport Depot, 1917

based on his letters

These are the best days I have ever had
since I enlisted, with the frostbite gone
melted with nights I thought I would go mad

into the horses, solid as their muck.
One leapt as I got on. Somehow I sat
each stiff-legged buck.

Then we bowled four horse wagons through the frost.
We passed the fields of Crécy, blind with light.
Nothing is lost.

A boy, I galloped Scarborough's sand. The dance
of hooves beat in my head. My long back sore,
I pound white roads of France.

How horses jar us, scar us, yet our rest
falls sweet as their oats' hiss.
Let my days pour.
These are the best.

No

No one is ever good enough,
or kind enough.
No one stays awake
through the lovely rush of rain which fills our dark.
No one can hold the music.
They are counting coins or frowning,
they are toppling, they are drowning.
No one is good.

But nothing is as quick as us,
no screen can match us,
tape's whirr catch us,
nothing tilts like sun
to light from sad.
Nothing in all history
can reach to take your hand from me,
the dark, the rain's gift, O
we should be glad.

Honeycomb

It is too beautiful to eat.
Knife crumbles it from gold to dark.
Our keenest edge cannot stay sharp
while in our walls, which seemed so strong,
damp murmurs with the evening sleet.
I wonder if I live too long

but then I taste the honeycomb,
its waxen white upon my teeth,
its liquid sun which hides beneath.
Small deities, of wind or moon,
behold me. In my shabby room
I am a god. I lick the spoon.

And

Sex is like Criccieth. You thought it would be
a tumble of houses into a pure sea
and so it must have been, in eighteen-ten.
The ranks of boarding houses marched up then.
They linger, plastic curtains at their doors,
or, more oddly, blonde ungainly statues.
The traffic swills along the single street
and floods the ears, until our feet
turn down towards the only shop for chips,
to shuffling queues, until sun slips
behind the Castle, which must be, by luck,
one of the few a Welsh prince ever took.
Or in the café, smoked with fat, you wait.
Will dolphins strike the sea's skin? They do not.

And yet, a giant sun nobody has told
of long decline, beats the rough sea to gold.
The Castle rears up with its tattered flag,
hand laces hand, away from valleys' slag.
And through the night, the long sea's dolphined breath
whispers into your warm ear, 'Criccieth'.

So

This is the trouble with spring. The snow comes down,
and it is all gone, under drift, dune, powder,
cats must be tunnelled for, dogs retrieved,
while milk is a dream, down the next street.

The cars stall on the hill.
Their wheels spin, then scream. The migrant jay
flashes for food. Blue is the wing
of the truant sky, soared Swiss, and pitiless.

How sudden the thaw is. Out of its burrow
the lawn creeps, tired but safe. The streets run smooth
    once more.
The cold no longer aches. At the end of a war,
your life limps home. And you are not sure that you
    want it.

8 a.m.

I am cycling, in a sensible, bright coat.
A girl comes pedalling quickly by, loose shawls
skidding from shoulders, hitched skirt, silver pumps.
I was that girl. O may she ride her falls.

Prologue

I need five hundred serious words. But still
the pure black kitten in an upstairs window
chases its tail, in ecstasy and boredom.
I cannot start till it falls off the sill.

Aftermath

I cleaned two homes. I learnt one thing.
What will survive of us is not
our careful words, our gardens' grace,
but rubber bands; green balls of string.

Vesta Tilley

(music hall star and recruiter)

Little Vesta had a mother
whom she would rarely see,
off touring with her father.
The dancing dog made three.

Her tiny shoes showed patent shine,
her shirts, a schoolboy's grace.
Her perfect tailored trousers
made the old Queen hide her face.

Vesta would claim her act was 'clean',
unlike that Marie Lloyd,
bedraggled, following the van.
Rich, sober, well-employed,

rocked only by the sudden night
her father's life was done,
little Vesta married
the theatre owner's son.

They stormed the States. They knocked on doors
which flustered women ran
to open, so her husband beat
that dreadful Labour man.

Though he was so much younger,
a foolish boy with flowers,
he died in Monte Carlo.
In rich blue empty hours

silent, she poured out memoirs,
twelve siblings; pro at six;
her father, cabs, the roaring halls,
Fathead the dog's sweet tricks.

What swelled her ruined throat with pride?
Her dearest trousered stunt,
the night she sent three hundred boys
straight to the Western Front.

Told

Ask everything you want to!
You cannot stay long.
No one, now, will ever hear
your father's father's songs.

I heard both songs and stories
from my mother's father's war.
But forty years from guns,
he grew a joyful liar.

He had seen every truce,
the football in the mud,
stood, he said, a batman, ironing,
to the great guns' thud.

No one else spoke of the mules,
led where no rail could run,
of axles, bubbling under mud
where useless wheels spun.

So every story ended
as his wife set cups for three,
'Then the mule kicked the Major –
so we laughed and drank our tea.'
Then the mule kicked the Major.
So we laughed, and drank our tea.

My Grandmother Said

It was the First World War.
Her husband was away.
She knew fear, but also found
new freedom in the day.

On Thursdays, with the farmer's wife,
old basket in her lap,
by butter slabs, she rode to Brigg,
shawled, in the pony trap.

Oh how I envied her!
I whined to Brigg by bus,
for school, no pony's dancing knees,
first sun in elder bush.

She would have crossed the Ancholme,
seen the canal glint wide.
She could buy apples and white thread,
jog home, to new moon's rise.

'But I was frozen, to my bones,
all winter.' Was that all?
My grandfather took up the reins.
She settled in her shawl.

Down Unwin's Track

And the rain stopped. And the sky spun
past the hills' flush of winter corn.
The mare strode out as though still young.

You walked. I almost said, last year
I saw a hare run with her young
just past the broken wall, just here.

Two flew in circles. First, one rose
upon its great back legs. It boxed
at air. The second flinched, then rose.

England has blackbirds, mice. To find
these strong black shapes makes the heart race,
as barley, under icy wind.

Boxing is courtship, failed. One broke,
tore past us to the rough safe hedge.
She crossed the sun. Her colours woke,

ears black, back russet, earth new-laid.
Her legs stretched straight. The late showers made
bright water fly from every blade.

Playground

Children, you lined up for your game;
one tall boy called, 'Sheep, sheep, come home.
The wolf has gone to Derbyshire.
He won't come back for seven years.'
You raced across the wind-blurred ground.
But he was wolf. He plunged, he pounced.
Each child, when he clutched coat or cuff,
straight-haired, scuff-toed, became the wolf.

Are you a wolf, grey, slender? Yet
as, elegantly, you stroll through
the café's buzz, the city's dome,
what is it you do not forget?
How even then they lied to you?
Still they sing out, 'Sheep, sheep, come home.'

Species

Sometimes they rise before me in the night:
the lemurs, eyes as bare and bright as moons;
the lizard, ancient as the afternoon;
the coral's tender hands which sun bleached white.
Some are immense: the tiger, shot and still;
some thumbnail-sized, like Chile's emerald frog
I never saw, and soon, nobody will.

Peelings

What am I good at? Useless things.
Listening to strangers on slow Scottish trains.
Did you know they had square sausages?
Standing on one leg – Not Yoga; muddy years of Wellingtons.
And peeling parsnips. Cooking grand Christmas dinner,
amongst dried cranberries, asparagus,
my daughter passed the knife, then was surprised
my awkward hands whipped smoothly down each root,
flicked pale gold slivers, thin, to save the flesh
which frost and soil had left as sweet as nuts,
which you may understand. And I remember
in tea's cold desert, though the saucepans steamed,
caught in a creaking visit once, I said,
(mouth full) 'These are good parsnips! Did you grow them?'
'Yes', said my father, shrunk to eighty years,
nodded with dignity, like his tall father.
We were not good with words. Each time my hand
slips down, as sharp as winter, and casts off
a pale coat, I am grateful, still, to parsnips.

Friday Afternoon

It was the autumn's last day, when the roof
was skimmed by wings – Red Admiral butterfly? –
a glance of black against the sky, like truth.

It was the day on which the goldfinch flung
its yellow wing against the glass, as though
it had drunk all the sweetness from the sun,

by which, in the wild garden, hips were seen
swelled by the last night's rain, crowns under leaves,
as though they could stay glossy, ever green,

a day when children played and did not fall
when traffic slowed to world's edge, a gold crawl,
which I heard, sun-lapped, sleeping through it all.

Poppy Seeds

Yes, they go everywhere, like breath.
They lodge in nails. They sweeten teeth,

strange food to me. Are they that haze,
red banks, once corn's, now motorways

or from some special flowers? I read
our newborn brain knows what we see

but not the words. They must be learned,
skilfully as these seeds were burned.

Oh, but I knew this. Before school
I spoke birds' nests, the blackbird's cool

mud, spoke eggs, the robin's scrawl.
I robbed no nest. The words took all.

Black seeds, the sweet sleep under grief,
give me the language of the leaf.

The Elms

We may know trees but rarely wood.
Elm was the workhorse, daily tree,
pale handle, for your fork and spade,
a chair as low as a bent knee
cut down for each uneven floor.
Women leaned into its curved back
as the milk pulsed, as birds once pressed
its crowded leaf, before storm's black.

The elms died fast, of one disease.
Is that a sapling, in the hedge?
No, hazel with its rose-flushed buds
then young lime with its heart-shaped edge.
Its step-grandchild must be the ash,
sprung on street corners, on stone hills,
until the lightning cracks the wind,
the crest is split, the fine twig spills.

But now ash has its own disease,
what can I still recall of elm?
Its seeds were white, softer than coins,
whose lack, or glut would overwhelm.
On other paths, by other trees,
I stand, still in that storm of snow.
From park, low hedge, your elms still rise.
Look at them well, before they go.

Christmas on the Radio

With breakfast come ironic song selections,
one crooner who has Mafia connections,
a black singer who longs for a white Christmas.
The station with the weather drowns in carols,
sung with a local and lugubrious gloom
from merrily on high. Outside this room

in the damp yard, I brush unending dark,
one thin trickle of birds' song, not the lark.
Robin, in ivy, starlings, in town roofs,
wet half-forgotten corners are the proof
these maddening, ever-burnished tunes ring right.
Now the sun sleeps. We wake to our own light.

Dickens: a daydream

The scrapman's son bangs at our door,
skives school, like father, grandfather,
all crammed in van's hum. 'Anything, sir?'
curls wild, your scavenging people.

The doe-eyed girl at the café till
is child's height, yet does not spill
one bean from heaped trays, hammers bills,
your frantic, stunted people.

Bad teeth, bent hips, the pitbull's snarl
called you out from the lawyer's yarns.
Happiness bored you most of all,
white tables, good, quiet people.

One was your wife. You glimpsed ahead
the young actress's breasts instead,
buds crushed by silk. She never said
your name, changed dates, fooled people.

London, in its lost party time,
the trees' lit snow, the towers' gold chime,
the heat of bars, the twist of lime,
you shun as in a fever.

We meet beneath the dripping bridge,
soot, fear and sorrow on each ledge.
Hurt child, you scour each rag-strewn beach,
walk all night, stride and shiver

until the dawn strikes London's walls
and clangs Good morning from St Paul's.
Waitresses, Poles, striped bankers pour,
your million words. Sleep, river.

Skies

It began, like wonder, back there
in the village's dark huddle
which I can never visit, like a star.

In high orbit, warm muddle,
my father's hard-packed arms, I passed.
Winter wind stilled, hedge and puddle

pure ice. Above my wreath of breath,
the weak eye of the one streetlight
beyond Back Lane and Temple Garth,*

skies pricked with white until the night
swam with its stars. In their grave blaze
they filled my gaze like wings in flight

which never left, unlike the house,
the anxious moves, my mother's care.
For years I stood by my own house

with books and charts. My father there
could only name the tilted Plough
he followed with the snorting pair.

But I found Pegasus, the slow
sweep of the Swan, a fierce red eye,
the Bull. I watched the Hunter go

with frost's belt, over towns where I
now lived, where, still, the galaxy
boiled by his sword in clouding sky.

The books are laid aside. I see
new roofs, more weak lamps. Whirled and free
the stars, my calm dead, walk with me.

*   'Temple' refers to the Knight Templars, who once controlled part of
the village's land. 'Garth', a Viking word, is used here of a farmyard.